COUNSELING MEN

CREATIVE PASTORAL CARE AND COUNSELING SERIES
Howard W. Stone and Howard Clinebell, coeditors

BOOKS IN THE SERIES

Counseling Men
Philip L. Culbertson

Crisis Counseling (Revised Edition)
Howard W. Stone

Integrative Family Therapy
David C. Olsen

Risk Management
Aaron Liberman and Michael J. Woodruf

Woman-Battering
Carol J. Adams

CREATIVE PASTORAL CARE AND COUNSELING

COUNSELING MEN

PHILIP L. CULBERTSON

FORTRESS PRESS   MINNEAPOLIS

To my children, Katie and Jacob,
who bear the hopes of the next generation
of men and women.

Library of Congress Cataloging-in-Publication Data

Culbertson, Philip Leroy, 1944–
    Counseling men / Philip L. Culbertson.
    p. cm. — (Creative pastoral care and counseling series)
    Includes bibliographical references.
    ISBN 0–8006–2786–5 (alk. paper)
    1. Men — Pastoral counseling of. 2. Church work with men.
I. Title.
BV639.M4C85 1994
259'.081 — dc20   94–2825
                                      CIP

Manufactured in the U.S.A.   AF 1–2786

98   97   96   95   94   1   2   3   4   5   6   7   8   9   10

CONTENTS

Foreword by Howard W. Stone   7

Preface   9

1. Gender-specific Listening Skills   11

2. Facing the Masculine Ego   22

3. Employment and Retirement   35

4. Being Parented, Being a Parent   46

5. Marriage and Communication   59

6. Love and Friendship Needs   73

7. Masculine Spirituality   83

Bibliography   93

FOREWORD

Counseling Men aims to help concerned men achieve a clearer identity in the whirlwind of change that is occurring in family and relationship structures. Philip Culbertson addresses the radical disparity between the stereotypes of how men are portrayed in our society and how they actually live their lives, between the media's macho, superhero, all-controlling, fantastic lovers and the fearful cogs in the wheel of today's impersonal business world, mortgaged to the hilt and worried about career and the responsibilities of providing for his family. This book is based on the liberation model which calls persons into the freedom of the future, helping them rise above the confines of past gender expectations.

Counseling Men, then, does not address every man's psychological need, but rather focuses on the typical concerns that men raise and how ministers— pastoral counselors, clergy, or commissioned laity—can fruitfully address these. For example, in chapter 1, gender-specific listening skills are discussed so that the minister, whether female or male, can tune into the language and worldview of men. Chapter 2 addresses the masculine ego, and ways that the minister can respond to it are suggested. Work and its importance in men's lives are the focus of chapter 3. Four losses are central when a man is retired or unemployed: income, daily structure, purpose, and identity. Chapters 4 and 5 concern marriage and being a parent. Chapter 6 addresses friendship, especially friendship between men. Finally, chapter 7 addresses masculine spirituality and makes suggestions about how this greatly ignored area can be developed.

In contrast to some of the other books in this series, whether published or under development, this book does not so much apply a method to a problem or issue as it formulates a perspective from which to understand the typical middle-class male worldview. The men being counseled here are not themselves dysfunctional (as in Carol Adams's *Woman-Battering,* for example), but their inadequate worldview—whether they are conscious of it or not—is under siege. Culbertson helps the reader understand that crumbling worldview so that appropriate empathy can be achieved.

Throughout, I found myself agreeing and demurring, but always being engaged by Culbertson's formulations. His ideas will provoke and comfort, sensitize and humanize those who take seriously the changing world in which men find themselves. This book is an important resource for those seeking to minister to men.

HOWARD W. STONE

PREFACE

Men are reaching out in increasing numbers for help, beset by changing expectations—both their own and what is expected of them. Beleaguered by professional or vocational lives that are increasingly abusive in a lagging economy, confused by rapidly changing family and relationship structures, and isolated by the assumed truisms as to what men are like, men are seeking places to speak, listen, and come to terms with change. Yet listening to men is not always easy for ministers. Men are presumed to have power and privilege, yet confess to ministers their exhaustion, isolation, failure, or lack of power.

This book offers a way of bridging such apparent contradictions by providing a liberation model for counseling men and encouraging their spiritual development—a large task, but a modest goal. A generation ago, Janet Radcliffe Richards wrote of the women's movement: "Feminism is not concerned with a group it wants to benefit, but with a type of injustice it wants to eliminate" (1980, 5). In contrast, much in the emerging men's movement seems focused on benefiting men—from assisting them in achieving a clearer identity in the midst of changing social arrangements, to seeking to redress so-called feminist-generated excesses. This book is not about redressing excesses; women are rightly concerned whenever men gather to find themselves (Thistlethwaite 1992, 418). But neither can this book achieve the larger goal of focusing on injustices to be eliminated, except in indirect ways.

By *liberation model* is meant the helpful distinction by James Griffiss (1985, 85-114) regarding how pastoral care has developed in the Christian tradition. The Constantinian model, which has dominated, was derived from the Logos Christology of the patristic period. It presupposes that the created order is now the order of redemption and salvation; Christian life is understood as the tranquil working-out of God's providence through the Spirit in the church. The role of the minister in the Constantinian model is to nudge the straying or disillusioned back into an affirmation of the social order, including hierarchies of power, as an expression of God's will. Christians are called to conform to authority, class, and gender-role structures as these are already perceived.

In contrast, the liberation model emerges from theological and political sensitivities. The New Testament gives large witness to the inbreaking of God's realm and the free working of the Spirit in the Christian community and the world. Meanwhile we are increasingly aware how unstable and unjust the present political orders are. In this model, persons are called into the free-

9

dom of the future, while social and ecclesiastical structures are viewed as tentative and revisable.

The resulting focus on community and future offers healthier ways of being for men. Not only do men need to be supported as they break the bonds of the powerful structures that unsettle and abuse them, but they also need freedom from the crippling stereotypes of masculinity they have inherited. A healthy Christian person, male or female, is one who is liberated from the oppressive expectations of gender behaviors (Clinebell 1976, 4). In this way, men are opened to God's love for who we are, not what we do (Augsburger 1986, 350). Throughout this book, the term *minister* is used to identify the ministers who mediate this liberation, whether they are pastoral counselors, clergy, or commissioned laypersons.

Acknowledgment for their individual contributions and encouragement during the development of this book is gratefully offered to Joe Ballard, Mark Biddle, Sally Brown, Michael Doty, Zev Gotthold, David Lott, Ken Love, Macacada, David May, Al Minor, Don Murphy, Jörg Neufang, Jim Pierson, Charlotte Pritchett, Jim Pritchett, Daniel Rossing, Janet Hall Valkovich, Minnie Warburton, Rebecca Abts Wright; to my editors at Fortress Press, Timothy Staveteig and Michael West; to Wanda Culbertson and to the John M. Allin Fellowship for underwriting the time out of my teaching schedule; and to Jacques Nicole, Margaret Koch, the staff and "angels" of the Institut Ecumenique, Chateau de Bossey, Switzerland, who gave me a place, both physically and emotionally, for writing this book.

1

GENDER-SPECIFIC LISTENING SKILLS

In his disturbing novel *Couples,* John Updike describes a confrontation between the protagonist, Piet, and his wife, Angela, when she asks to seek professional help because their marriage is falling apart. Piet begins:

> "What's your stake in all this hocus-pocus with egos and ids? Why are you so defensive? I suppose you want to go to a psychiatrist too."
> "Yes."
> "The hell you will. Not as long as you're my wife."
> "Oh? You're thinking of getting another wife?"
> "Of course not. But it's very insulting. It implies I don't give you enough sex."
> (1968, 232)

Piet fears that if his wife goes for psychiatric assistance, it can mean only that he is not "man enough" to keep her happy.

Such an exchange raises several questions. Are women and men truly different from each other? Does a minister need to be concerned about listening to men in one way and to women in another? On many levels, women and men are probably more alike than dissimilar, and it is wise to be suspicious of divergences based solely on sex. We are all born of the same biological processes, eat, desire community in some form, and we share an urge to leave behind some legacy—whether children or works of art or a cleaner earth.

Yet, the fields of biomedical research, psychology, communication linguistics, and behavioral and cultural anthropology suggest that men and women function in different ways. Their brains and hormones appear to work differently, although some of the experiments supporting such conclusions are flawed as Carol Tavris (1992) has shown. Women and men respond in different ways emotionally, although how much of this difference is the result of enculturation rather than biological mechanism is not clear. Men have much higher rates of suicide, alcoholism, homelessness, and crime; men of color show even higher rates (Kimbrell 1991, 66-67), suggesting cultural more than biological mechanisms at work.

CULTURAL FORCES

Deborah Tannen (1990) has made famous the communication differences between the genders. Perhaps the cultural context can account for many of the reasons that to use Tannen's example (15), a man would interpret a question as a request for information whereas a women would raise a question as an opportunity to negotiate the needs of each.

With overwhelming frequency, the movie and television media portray men as abusers, heroes, sex objects, or buffoons. Pat Conroy's emotionally abusive father in *The Great Santini*, Sebastian who manipulates both women and men in Tennessee Williams's *Suddenly Last Summer*, the heroic antics of Mel Gibson and Danny Glover in *Lethal Weapon*, the sexual prowess of the contestants in the Fox Network's "Studs" or the incompetent buffoon on ABC's "Home Improvement," the mindless male violence of *Boyz 'n the Hood*, the brutes my own son loves so much in the World Wrestling Federation, the amazing adventures of *Indiana Jones*, the taunting cruelty of the young soldiers in *Casualties of War*, the seductive chiseled men of cosmetic advertising—these are the stereotypes that daily confront men in our society. Such images may offer men the opportunity to live out many of their secret fantasies of prowess and success, but at the same time they remind men over and over of how humdrum their daily lives are, how vulnerable they are to the power of others, and how little hope they really have to measure up to the images of manhood dangled before them in the media.

Andrew Kimbrell pictures the disjuncture between how men are portrayed and who men know themselves to be:

> Modern men are entranced by this simulated masculinity—they experience danger, independence, success, sexuality, idealism, and adventure as voyeurs. Meanwhile, in real life most men lead powerless, subservient lives in the factory or office—frightened of losing their jobs, mortgaged to the gills, and still feeling responsible for supporting their families. Their lauded independence—as well as most of their basic rights—disappear the minute they report for work. The disparity between their real lives and the macho images of masculinity perpetrated by the media confuses and confounds many men. (1991, 70)

Even though the relative privilege of most males, especially white men, is not to be ignored, most men feel themselves to be the victims of structures (racist, classist, and sexist) spinning out of control. These structures are premised on a self-perpetuating cadre of powerful white men exploiting the talents and energies of less-privileged white men, persons of color, women, the poor and disenfranchised, the structures of our economy, and the limited natural resources of our environment. In my experience, this patriarchal power not only creates much pain in our world but also drives many people—including men—to ministers for a listening ear.

David Augsburger (1986, 217) defines patriarchalism as the product of four interlocking premises: first, that male physical strength is a part of intended natural law; second, that families and societies are naturally based on aggression, domination, procreation, and spouse and child protection; third, that property, production, and the distribution of goods are the natural domain of men; and fourth, that male superiority, dominance, and privilege are a part of received religious revelation. These four interlocking justifications—biological, cultural, economic, and religious—have provided until recently an unquestioned position for the domination of half the world's people by the other half (Iglitzin and Ross, 1976, 15). Such patriarchal beliefs are oppressive by definition because they are premised on the domination of one gender over the other (Freire 1970, 40).

EXCAVATING MEN'S FEELINGS

Opposition against patriarchy has emerged on several fronts, including feminist, womanist, African-American, Hispanic, and other critiques. With the advent of the men's movement, the term *men* has taken on two different meanings: (1) those who are taking seriously the criticisms of patriarchy and are seeking a new identity, and (2) others who think that the dominant culture needs to be perpetuated. (The *men's movement* refers to the former group.) Thus, the distinction is sometimes made between traditionalist men and profeminist men, or new men.

Most men have been trained in their families of origin to suppress deeply their feelings and emotions. Even for men in the men's movement, recovering awareness of feelings and emotions can be difficult, especially when these men are in crisis and decide they need professional help. Michele Bograd notes:

> When women therapists are asked to generate a quick list of adjectives that describe male clients, they choose manipulative, hostile, intellectualizing, passive, distant, rigid, dominating, childlike, and generally uninterested in change. . . . Some men try to control therapy by yelling, storming out of sessions, refusing to speak, or aggressively engaging in intellectual argument. More subtly, but no less powerfully, they clench their fists, flush, or breathe irregularly. (1990, 56)

These behaviors, according to Bograd, are not typical of women clients. Rather they are behaviors that men adopt in order to avoid having to dig deeply inside themselves for feelings and emotions.

Men resist therapeutic work because they have been taught to associate feelings and emotions with femininity and, in the course of cultivating a masculine identity, have worked hard to eradicate all traces of femininity within themselves. Patriarchal masculinity denigrates and trivializes the world of inner experience, feeling, and intuition. This inner world is deemed weak, making men too vulnerable. Men have been taught to value independence over interrelatedness, measurable objectivity over inner reality, linearity over the circular character of emotionality.

Men who have begun to value their own inner world are sometimes called soft men. *Soft* is the term that women generally do not use about men. In *Iron John*, Robert Bly uses the term accusatorially, and he is correct that most men register it as derogatory. Soft challenges the manner in which another man acts out his masculinity, implying that he is neither hard nor aggressive enough. (The phallic overtones of the derogation are so obvious that further comment is not needed.) To insult a man, simply call him a woman. In contrast, women are often praised for being soft—thus revealing how low women are held in some men's esteem and how deeply these men fear being identified as feminine. This fear of being called a woman can quickly spill over into *misogyny,* the hatred of things associated with women.

To be hard, to prove one's male superiority, to protect against the feared feminine, emotional repression is passed from father to son. This repression makes male emotional health an elusive chimera unless the assumptions behind the masculine persona are brought to light. When feelings are repressed over and again, they fester until they become "nightmares of pain" (Hopcke 1990, 22).

To secure healing, men need to find the courage to open their eyes to their inner landscape and their psychic surroundings, to force the resurrection of entire parts of themselves that have been denied or dead for years, to honor feelings as being as valuable as measurable external reality. The work is painful and slow; many men refuse to participate, calling forth instead the sort of reactions that Bograd and other therapists describe.

FORGETTING THEIR OWN BODIES

Men who have repressed feelings and emotions seem to be less aware of their bodily health and well-being needs. Ironically, men's bodies seem to require more care than women's. Jerome Kagan reports that boys—because they are more vulnerable than girls to stress of any kind—are much more likely to have aggression problems, neurotic symptoms, phobias, difficulty with toilet training, and learning handicaps. The mortality rate for male babies, for example, is much higher than that for female babies, although the reasons for this are not known. Reading disabilities are seven times more common in boys than in girls (Francke 1983, 41). Yet even though males begin life physically more vulnerable than females, they are soon acculturated to ignore the needs of their bodies and instead to concentrate on accomplishment and superior athletic ability by ignoring pain, by deadening sensory perceptions and emotions.

Patriarchy has traditionally promoted misogyny and *homophobia*—the hatred of things believed to be imitative of women. Both attitudes betray men's enormous discomfort with the human body, and patriarchs are the unwitting victims (along with women and gays) of the denial of that which is not masculine (feelings, emotions, and soft bodies). Not surprisingly, men are more likely than women to continue going to work when they are ill and statistically much less likely to see a physician for routine physical self-care and preventive medicine. Men, at the suggestion that they are disembodied, often counter with jokes about the superiority of the male physique (especially male genitalia) or with an insistence on their own self-pride. Pride of self, coupled with a failure to care for their bodies medically, proves that men are disembodied selves, so proud that they fail to see the indispensability of caring for their most familiar physical dwellings. Thus, bodies and body image are clearly gender-specific issues for ministers working with men.

RESISTING HELP

Because men are often emotionally repressed and trained not to care about their physical selves, getting them to ministers who might provide some help and support in their confusion or crisis can be difficult. Many men assume that counseling is a waste of time or that it implies weakness or failure. Some men find that talking intimately with a male minister raises the specter of homophobia. Other men find that talking with a female minister threatens their manhood.

A man will often wait to seek help until his crisis has resulted in some sort of destruction—perhaps the breakup of his family or loss of his job because of emotional flare-ups or the ruination of his health through neglect or chemical addiction. Statistically, psychotherapists see many more women patients than men, not because women are more troubled, but because fewer men will recognize when they themselves are in difficulty.

Ministers are painfully aware that when a marriage becomes deeply troubled, the wife is likely to seek support and counsel, whereas in more than one-half of the cases, the husband refuses to join her in seeking help. Apart from an inability of men to care for themselves, three factors explain this imbalance.

First, formal counseling is often conducted in a language that men have been conditioned to reject. When first reaching down inside themselves to find feelings, many men conclude that they have none. When asked to answer the question, How do you feel? many men will begin by saying, I think that. . . . The minister needs to help men understand that *I think* is not an answer to a feeling question. Later, when men discover feelings, they may not know how to name them. A skilled minister knows how to suggest softly some possible names—needy, sad, hurt, scared—although men seeking care need to be urged to name feelings on their own. The feelings that the minister will encounter first are probably anger and loneliness (Rosenberg 1983, 12).

Second, a cry for help registers with many men as a failure to be independent. If a man is dependent, he usually judges himself as a failure. This odd resistance is one of the by-products of the individuation process that men undergo at an early age, in which they reject in a firm and exaggerated manner whatever smacks of the feminine in order to establish their own masculine identity. The refusal to ask for help takes many forms in addition to the fear of entering counseling. For example, many men will not stop to ask for directions when they are lost on a trip, and others will not read the directions for assembly when putting together some new purchase.

Third, formal counseling yields results only slowly over a long period of time, and many men are conditioned not to be patient with drawn-out processes that have no visible results or measurability. Men are likely to want to see something tangible quickly, some product that would make sense in the business world, something that satisfies their constant hunger for achievement. Yet the counseling process seldom brings quick results; as one therapist has observed, "I find myself often devoting the better part of the first year of therapy simply to the development of a workable emotional awareness" (Hopcke 1990, 12).

THREE GENDER-SPECIFIC TASKS

Because of this masculine resistance, three tasks prove necessary for men in counseling that are usually less needed for women. Any of these tasks can provide the entry point into the complicated system of a man's long-suppressed feelings. These tasks are not always part of the professionally recommended relationship between a therapist and a patient. Pastoral care and counseling, however, is a different process from formal therapy because pastoral care grows out of the kind of support and involvement that Christian women and men are called to offer one another. Nevertheless, all ministers should heed the cautions given.

Modeling Emotions

Studies of men's conversation patterns reveal that men generally limit their conversation to five topics: sports, politics, women, their professional successes, and toys (such as guns, boats, computers, and stereos). These are not likely to be productive topics in providing care for men, but many men have little experience in discussing other subjects, and so they seem inarticulate. Thus, listening to men may involve patiently teaching the vocabulary of emotions and offering specific exercises in communication.

Part of such teaching is modeling the expression of emotions. The minister may share part of his or her own experience or personal journey. Such sharing needs to be done in a manner that keeps the man in crisis the focus of concern, rather than the minister. Certainly the minister cannot trade away effectiveness by becoming so familiar with the counselee that impartiality is sacrificed. But, if a man is having difficulty finding his deeply buried emotions and even more in naming them, then the minister might tell a story that parallels the careseeker's situation and, in the course of telling it, describe the emotions that the minister felt at the time.

An even simpler technique is to offer sound-bites, such as, If that were happening to me, I would feel _____ . Is that how you are feeling? In this manner, the minister can suggest empathy with the careseeker, teach him when the expression of feeling is appropriate or inappropriate, model the naming of emotions, and generally encourage a climate in which the careseeker feels safe to explore parts of himself long repressed.

Choosing the Topics

Sometimes the minister needs to choose topics of conversation that seem abstract enough not to threaten. Some of the literature from the men's movement builds discussions of identity upon the archetypes and heroes typical to Jungian therapy, such as the king, the warrior, the magician, the lover. In this literature, men are encouraged to find, say, the king within themselves and then to appropriate the good qualities of the king as a part of their changing identity. These archetypes and heroes are often illustrated by classical mythologies, such as the feats of Odysseus, the foolishness of Pan, the heroism of King Arthur, or the journey to maturity of Iron John, which Robert Bly has drawn so effectively.

Even though conversations about heroes and archetypes with their more objective focus can make men more comfortable talking about themselves, most archetypes offer both a positive model for identity formation and a dark side. Susan Brooks Thistlethwaite writes:

> Archetypes of King, Warrior, Magician, or Lover themselves give very mixed messages. Even though in Western culture the move away from royalist forms of government is associated with advancing democracy, we are now asked to believe that King is a nurturing, creative, protective image. The same is especially true of the warrior image: the aggressive, "world-building" energy of twentieth-century warriors, among them, the generals Patton and MacArthur, great strategists, men of great courage, and men devoted to causes greater than their own personal survival. . . . The warrior archetype in particular makes me very nervous. I feel it gives tacit permission for men to idolize violence, and that this will inevitably find expression, as it has historically done, in rape, battering, and war making. (1992, 418)

I share Thistlethwaite's concern about the potential for men visiting violence on women based on these archetypes. In particular, I have expressed my concern about the sexism inherent in many archetypes (Culbertson 1993). Suffice it to say that the distance is not great between the king and the autocratic and irrational domination of the philosophy that "a man's home is his castle."

Setting Rules

Some ministers make themselves available outside any formal counseling situation. In a few instances when a man is in crisis, the minister may find it helpful to involve the man in some joint project, such as assisting a youth group in a bowling tournament or making home repairs for elderly persons or leading a Saturday morning workshop on automobile maintenance. Prior to such occasion, setting the rules—the expectations—is important.

Setting rules also needs to be done during counseling or caregiving times. These can be stated in a clear, firm, but nonangry manner as needed. One rule might be, for example, that threats against others will not be tolerated. Within limits, it may be necessary for the minister to become confrontative with men whose feelings are intransigently repressed. It may be effective to hold up to a man the mirror of his own sexism or to confront him about the ways in which he is dependent on women to do his emotional work or even to expose his assumptions that women are necessarily interested in meeting his needs.

USING A NONSEXIST APPROACH

In order to model emotions and choose topics, the minister might find a non-sexist approach to counseling helpful (Rawlings and Carter 1977, 51-54). By nonsexist is meant that the minister is asked to focus on a recognition of his or her own cultural biases, affirm the variety among men and women who seek help, and remain open regarding gender-role reversals. (*Gender role* is the manner in which a person behaves in order to let others in a society know that he or she wishes to be perceived as embodying the presumed characteristics of a particular gender.) This method views ministers themselves as victims of socially inherited gender-role constructs. Six assumptions frame this approach.

1. The minister should remain aware of his or her own values, especially as they relate to expectations for maleness and femaleness. Because studies suggest that those in helping professions are subject to the same biases as all other people in that culture, the minister may need special training to learn to let go of these biases. The careseeker's options should be limited as little as possible by the prejudices of the minister.
2. Differences from the assumed societal norm in a careseeker's gender-role behavior need to be viewed in the best possible light, given the particular situation. Choices need to be made on the basis of what might work best for the careseeker and other persons affected, regardless of society's "shoulds" in relation to gender-role behavior.
3. The desired behavioral outcome for all careseekers is the ability to choose adaptively and live with personal integrity. The minister need not be overly concerned about reversals in gender-role predisposition. That is, if a man wishes to sew clothes (or a woman wants to change the oil in her car), then this choice represents nothing more than appropriate adaptation to the individual's skills and interests.
4. Females and males need to be viewed as individuals who are gendered, rather than genders struggling to be individuals. Females are seen as capable of the same autonomy and assertiveness as males, and males are seen as capable of the same expressiveness and tenderness as females.
5. The minister avoids using any power inherent in her or his role to reinforce or punish behavior that appears to be decidedly "masculine" in a woman, or "feminine" in a man, according to social norms.
6. Careseeker and minister need to work cooperatively to achieve the values and choices appropriate for the careseeker in this situation.

The goal of nonsexist therapy is to transcend gender-role expectations and their resulting oppression. The value of adopting this approach when counseling men is twofold. First, any oppression or confusion that a man is experiencing does not get reinforced through the counseling relationship. This benefit is of particular importance when the minister is also a male because in a male-male counseling situation, the unconscious danger is to slip back into a sexist, traditionally masculine mentality. Second, this style allows the minister to model an emotional sensitivity and choose a broader set of topics.

MINISTERS AND GENDER

Often, ministers need unusual patience in working with men, especially at the beginning of the counseling relationship. "I was having Nick's feelings for him, often the first step in therapy with men alienated from their emotional life" (Hopcke 1990, 41). At times when a man in crisis approaches a minister, he is seeking whomever is available to offer support and clarification. At other times, the man will make a conscious choice whether he would prefer to relate to a male or a female minister. The minister needs to decide whether it might be productive to explore this selection issue. In any case, the minister needs to keep in mind the different dynamics between a same-gender counseling relationship and an opposite-gender one. These dynamics often constitute issues around which the relationship rules can be set.

Women as Ministers

When a female minister listens to a male careseeker, she will often experience a set of reactions that are not countertransference or family-of-origin issues, but have more to do with the way in which she has been conditioned to allow gender roles to structure intimate relationships. Michele Bograd (1990, 52) suggests some helpful questions a female minister might need to ask herself in order to identify areas of interference in the counseling relationship:

- What kind of behavior by a man sets me off? What words and behaviors are at the core of my present responses?
- As a woman growing up, what was I taught about men and how women should take care of them?
- Do I feel equally strong and nurturant with male and female careseekers? What makes for any difference?
- In what ways do I respond differently to men in my personal life as compared with men in my ministry?

Few ministers, male or female, can counteract a lifetime's conditioning about the ways that men and women are expected to respond to each other. Because such responses are often manipulative, excessively dependent, or theatrical, ministers need to devote attention to making themselves aware of the personal dangers that arise to interfere with any relationship requiring empathy and insight.

Men as Ministers

When a male minister listens to a male careseeker, he faces some of the same issues as does a female as well as others that are unique to a male-male relationship. For example, male ministers need to ask themselves how they have been enculturated to respond to other men. Two themes recur in the recent men's movement literature regarding the male-male counseling relationship: (1) a male careseeker often has unconscious desires to work out unresolved problems with his father; and (2) strange tensions (from himself or the minister) are likely to surface when the male minister seems to be less than manly, using the vocabulary of feelings and emotions.

Transference (also known as *cathexis*), in Freudian terminology, means the projection of one's feelings about someone onto someone else. The person on whom the feelings are transferred often resembles the absent person in some way. Because of the presumed role of the minister's authority, the careseeker may transfer (cathect) on him or her unresolved feelings from his childhood about the same-gender parent. Particularly common are men in crisis who transfer feelings about their fathers onto male ministers. A counseling context may take advantage of transference in order to surface emotions and feelings that can be analyzed. But the male minister needs to guard against *countertransference* — projecting his own feelings from previous relations, such as unrelieved memories of an authoritarian father or other abusive patriarch, back onto the careseeker.

Related to transference is the bind that many male ministers experience when counseling a man. On the one hand, the man is present because he wants help from some authority — an awkward request for many men to make. On the other hand, the assistance presented to him seems feminine, even effeminate — expressing emotions and focusing on relationships. This can create an air of mistrust, especially if the careseeker fears his own homosexual stirrings. The minister should not be concerned with proving his own masculinity to the careseeker, but with helping the careseeker toward health by challenging the underlying prejudices about what behaviors and styles of communication (gender roles) are appropriately masculine.

MINISTRY AND GENDER

An emerging issue in pastoral theology and ministry is the extent to which the minister needs to have experienced the careseeker's specific issues in order to offer effective ministry or pastoral care. To be sure, having recovered from physical abuse or alcohol addiction or cancer can improve the minister's understanding and approach when working with those whose similar wounds are fresh. But the concept of human empathy has sometimes been strained to the limit by the growing assumption that a minister needs to have "been there" before she or he can be helpful to others.

Can only women counsel women, or only men understand men? Any assumption that people of the same gender have had the same experiences, felt similar pain, and identify with each other more deeply is both true and false: true in those rare instances of shared experience and insight, but fallacious as a general assumption. Three reasons for this come to mind.

First, a bond of solidarity between two women or between two men is not necessarily easier to create than any other human bond. Every attachment between two people requires voluntary empathy and interpathy (the reciprocity of shared loving empathy). Such feelings are not necessarily available on demand.

Second, the so-called natural understandings of members of the same sex do not possess any virtue. In fact, such understandings are as problematic as they are advantageous, and no more likely to point out what is essentially responsible and causative of the pain experienced. Clear, tested, reflective insight and experience from a person of the same or different gender are far more important than simple identification.

Third, such identification frequently hinders growth because sympathy based on similarities reinforces pain by joining the other rather than transcending and inviting transcendence (Augsburger 1986, 236-37).

The crucial factors seem not to be gender, but (1) clear consciousness of the life situation of the other, (2) a capacity to discern influences internal and external to the person, (3) sensitivity to another's life experience, and (4) an understanding of interpersonal dynamics. Men's listening to men holds different rewards from women's listening to men, but the issue of the minister's gender is less important than the level of the skill and experience she or he brings to the relationship and her or his willingness to offer nonsexist counseling that supports and is appropriate to the needs of men in crisis. The unself-examined male or female minister may find the pitfalls of counseling men too seductive to evade; ministers still trapped in patriarchally defined gender roles and expectations are of little use to men in transition and confusion. Counseling men demands perceptive ministers who are committed to the transcendence of gender stereotypes and the liberation of both women and men from oppressions and manipulations that hold them back from living into the fullness and health of God's love for the humbled and powerless.

2

FACING THE MASCULINE EGO

Gavin approached Charles, the lay pastor at his church, in an angry mood. When Charles asked Gavin what was troubling him, Gavin railed about the "gossipy feminists who are always putting men down." Charles was quickly swept up in agreeing with Gavin about how irritating it was to be the subject of derision.

But as the conversation settled into the frequent pattern of male versus female, them against us, Charles returned to his earlier question: exactly what had angered Gavin? Without hesitation, Gavin indicated that his own wife, Harriet, was the chief offending feminist. Surprised at this bald criticism, Charles kept focusing on the prompting event.

For months, Gavin admitted, he had been sexually impotent with his wife. Because Harriet was confused about what was wrong, she had talked in confidence to her best friend, who had then told her husband, who told someone else, and before long Gavin was the brunt of a golf partner's joke that he "wasn't quite the man we thought you were."

A moment of silence ensued as both men stared at the floor. Gavin's anger at "gossipy feminists," Charles concluded, was only a cover for his shame at being impotent, "not quite a man," as Gavin had said. Then Charles referred Gavin to a physician. Charles had nearly fallen into the trap of traditional men's talk about women, and his earlier complicity in gender stereotyping embarrassed him.

LOOKING AT THE MAN'S FACE

If men are as powerful as many claim, what can explain men's quickness to feel shame at women's critique of masculine behavior? An approximate answer is that in such situations, men experience social denigration, loss in the advance of others, belittlement.

Shame is sometimes described as loss of face. The word *face* has three senses as a verb: to encounter (face to face), to overlay (to face a wall with brick), or to address (to face up to a matter). The minister's task follows each sense; namely, the minister needs to look at the man and observe how this man is covering up his fragile ego. Then the minister needs to assist the man in addressing the source of his fears and sense of fragility.

Seeing the Man's Role

David Augsburger defines face as one's "personal integrity, good character, and the confidence of society and of oneself in one's ability to play one's social role" (1986, 132). A person is said to lose face when he or she falls short of role expectations assigned by society or violates rules of conduct or breaks communal customs. The resulting judgment is directed toward the offender and his or her whole family.

"The concept of 'face' . . . is a universal concern of human beings, who live not only by their self-esteem but by esteem reflected from the faces of others" (133). Preserving face is an attempt to protect the way one is viewed by those whom society grants the authority to stand in judgment upon one's social position and worth, including the power of self-judgment one adopts internally. Such loss of face can occur whenever an embarrassing secret is revealed or one is slandered or caught in a compromising situation, as in driving while intoxicated.

Shame is the end product of losing face. Shame names what one feels when society is perceived to have decided that one has failed to measure up to standards, including gender-role behavior or professional authority or personal responsibility. Consciously or not, many men respond to life through choices and behaviors motivated by the fear of being caught or shamed.

Discerning the Man's Shame

Shame, like embarrassment, comes in many forms, but unlike embarrassment regarding, say, a spilled cup of coffee, shame endures as a profound condition, often with long-term consequences. Whereas embarrassment is manifested in red ears and a flushed face, shame is often hidden as a deep sense of unredressable pain. Lowell Noble (1975, 4–6) has distinguished varieties of shame as to whether the community or the individual is passing judgment and what the character of that judgment is. These categories can be adapted as follows:

- Innocent shame: Feeling injured when one's character is defamed without justification.
- Guilty shame: Feeling incompetent before others when one is exposed as having violated an ethical norm of the community or having acted hypocritically.
- Social shame: Feeling embarrassed when one makes a social blunder or error.
- Familial shame: Feeling disgraced because of the behavior of another family member.
- Handicap shame: Feeling incomplete or disfigured regarding some bodily defect or physical imperfection.
- Discrimination shame: Feeling downgraded when treated as socially, racially, ethically, religiously, or vocationally inferior.

- Modesty or sexual shame: Feeling indecent and exposed when having unwittingly violated sexual, social, or dress norms and having done pro-scribed behavior.
- Inadequacy shame: Feeling marked, inferior, or inadequate from passiv-ity, repeated failure, or abuse.
- Public shame: Feeling the community's open ridicule as punishment or as a result of group pathology.
- Anticipated shame: Fear of being exposed for any planned or desired be-havior that would result in self-condemnation or public shaming.

Even though this list is narrowly defined and not comprehensive, it shows the complexity of shame feelings and the power that the threat of losing face can have over any woman or man. When counseling men, the skilled minister needs to remain alert to the shame and saving-face issues that lurk beneath the surface of the careseeker's complaints and reactions.

OBSERVING THE FACE OF SHAME

Patriarchs threaten other men (and women) with their power, especially the power of shame. Although shame is only one of the three types of awareness that propel people into counseling—guilt and anxiety being the other two—shame is the leading propellant for men. Shame, guilt, and anxiety, however, are not easily distinguished from each other. Picture a man who is divorcing his wife. What does he feel? He may feel guilt over his own actions or choices during the marriage. He may feel anxiety about whether he will be able to meet his own personal needs in the weeks ahead. He will surely feel shame, or loss of face, over being a part of a marriage that has failed the expectations brought to it by the couple and society.

What does a father who is moving out of the home feel in relation to the children he is leaving behind? He may feel guilt over his choice to live else-where. He may feel anxiety for his children's emotional and financial future. He will surely feel shame over having failed society's and his own expecta-tions of what a father should be—a successful provider and protector.

If the man has a son, what does the son feel in relation to the father who has abandoned him in the course of a divorce? The son may feel the sort of guilt that assumes the divorce is his fault. He may feel anxiety about his fi-nancial future or the loss of a confidant and role model. But he will surely feel shame because he is an involuntary part of a family that has been broken. Even when divorce is common in society, studies show that children have great difficulty in telling someone else that their parents are divorced—because the statement makes them feel shamed.

Procreator, Protector, Provider

The concept of face explains a man's deep fear of being revealed personally, stripped naked before the judgment of the public eye as to his effectiveness as an employee or professional colleague, but even more so as a husband, a father, a man. He is expected to be (and expects himself to be) procreator, protector, and provider. A man's form of nurturing others is captured in these traditional roles. Regarding their positive aspects, David Gilmore writes:

> Women nurture others directly . . . "real" men nurture too, although they would perhaps not be pleased to hear it put this way. Their support is indirect and thus less easy to conceptualize. Men nurture their society by shedding their blood, their sweat, and their semen, by bringing home food for both child and mother, by producing children, and by dying if necessary in faraway places to provide a safe haven for their people. This, too, is nurturing in the sense of endowing or increasing. (1990, 229)

By custom, a man exercises his appropriate place in society when he is procreating, protecting, and providing. These roles remain appropriate even for feminist-sensitive men as long as the roles are defined in a manner that does not provoke violence of any sort toward any person.

Social Expectations as Sources of Fear

Procreating, protecting, and providing have negative dimensions. When viewed as exclusively the power domain of males, an entitlement naturally or divinely warranted, they become the justification for patriarchal oppression. The masculinity of men is then judged by how well they discharge these roles; women are denied full humanity because they cannot fulfill these roles (for example, when procreator is defined too narrowly as impregnator). Young boys are taught to sacrifice in order to achieve these ideals. Frank Pittman describes the "invisible male chorus of all the other guys who hiss or cheer as he attempts to approximate the masculine ideal. . . . The chorus is made up of all the guy's comrades and rivals, all his buddies and bosses, his male ancestors and his male cultural heroes, his models of masculinity—and above all, his father" (1990, 42). Indeed, the majority of males live lives haunted by the voices of these males, past and present.

This patriarchal chorus is the history of men's contest with women for pride of place. Men's lives are haunted by this ancient and noisy drone as the fear of being shamed—failing to live up to the expectations that society and its patriarchs have taught them. Many men would like to squelch, even silence, this chorus, but they are afraid.

The Fear of Seeming "Feminine"

Protecting their role as procreator, protector, and provider sets up a tension, even hostility, from men toward women that is animated by men's fear of being mistaken for women, or being equal with women. Anthony Astrachan in *How Men Feel* describes this fear poignantly:

> Some men take the idea of equal value between men and women, or the mere possibility of higher value for women, as part of a threat that we will become like women or indeed be transformed into women. Even without the often misinterpreted concepts of penis envy and castration fear, the fear of becoming like women can lead to a sense of shame in men. (1986, 30)

Astrachan points out that men's fear of being mistaken for women is a fear of becoming "like the other." Theologically and psychologically, it is an accepted truism that human beings become persons, or individuate, only in relationship to an Other or others. This was Martin Buber's basic tenet in his seminal work, *I-Thou,* and in general, Judaism understands the proper human relationship to God as a mixture of cleaving love *(ahavah)* and distancing awe *(yirah).* Indeed, as much as we are drawn into loving another, we seem also to fear anything that is "other" than we are because we understand it even less than we understand ourselves.

The possibility of being confused with Other-as-Woman is one source of men's fear of shame. When men get locked into believing that their masculinity is proven by how far they have differentiated from women, how much they are like other men, and how they have measured up to the socially accepted definitions of procreator, protector, and provider, they are in need of liberation from both their own culture and themselves.

The Fear of Losing

Contests and games are based on strategies that lead to someone's winning while everyone else loses, or at least takes no higher than second place. Frank Pittman describes the centrality of gamesmanship in the formation of male identity: "[Men] see everything in life as a contest they must win. They can become workaholics or street fighters or sports fans, and busy themselves with the male-to-male games, which seem safer than games women want them to play" (1990, 49).

Games may be the place for teamwork, but even teamwork is still premised on an opponent's loss. A contest has one clear winner and a clear set of losers. Nothing is left open to subjective interpretation. Men's games are not the place for mutual care, interdependence, or ambiguity. Nor do games and contests have room for much creativity; they are played according to set rules, although one may strive creatively to use the rules to one's advantage. The research of Carol Gilligan (1982) and Jean Baker Miller (1976) emphasizes how typically masculine this win-at-all-costs paradigm is, for girls develop altogether different and more cooperative patterns of play.

Viewing the world as a cosmic venue of rules and contests, winning and losing, and insisting that procreation, protection, and provision are superior activities to women's nurturing, men fall victim to what is sometimes called "boy psychology" as opposed to "man psychology." To succeed in such a world without losing face, a man must live his life and conduct his relationships by assuming cutthroat competitiveness and the ever-present threat of losing. Deborah Tannen uses somewhat different terminology to describe this traditional masculine view of life in summarizing an argument she had with her husband about whether a third party's comments on her work should have been taken as a challenge or not:

> Having done the research that led to this book, I now see that my husband was simply engaging in the world in a way that many men do: as an individual in a hierarchical social order in which he was either one-up or one-down. In this

world, conversations are negotiations in which people try to achieve and maintain the upper hand if they can, and protect themselves from others' attempts to put them down and push them around. Life, then, is a contest, a struggle to preserve independence and avoid failure.

I, on the other hand, was approaching the world as many women do: as an individual in a network of connections. In this world, conversations are negotiations for closeness in which people try to seek and give confirmation and support, and to reach consensus. They try to protect themselves from others' attempts to push them away. Life, then, is a community, a struggle to preserve intimacy and avoid isolation. Though there are hierarchies in this world too, they are hierarchies more of friendship than of power and accomplishment. (1990, 24–25)

Men's competitive drive is not always the product simply of testosterone levels. It may also mask men's fear of losing face and its consequences. If a man can accumulate enough "points" by winning often enough, perhaps his vulnerabilities and almost-inevitable shaming will seem less significant. Such an approach is illusory, of course. Many a promising political candidate has been drummed out of the running on the basis of one scandal. Nonetheless, the fragile masculine ego remains invested in the hope that it can exercise a certain damage control in advance of being shamed by means of accumulating an impressive collection of prior winnings.

The Fear of Ambiguity

Psychologist Alfred Adler used the term *oppositional thinking* to describe an approach to the world that ruled out ambiguity and creativity: things are this way, or that way, and there is no room between them for partials, subtlety, compromise, or reconciliation. Adler deemed this manner of thinking to be a form of arrested development, the way a child thinks, not the way a mature adult thinks. Some men (and some women) carry their oppositional thinking into adulthood without stopping to examine it. In many cases, ideas of right and wrong are forms of oppositional thinking that ignore the many positions between the two extremes. Men's fear of being wrong—in an argument, in their public behavior or dress or attitudes, in the conduct of relationships—is an expression of the same immature approach to identity issues. Christian ministers are challenged to work with men toward a greater sophistication in their moral and ethical choices, and to a lessened investment in always being right.

Ministers may have their own homework to do in the arena of simplistic approaches to life in the faith. The church has traditionally perpetuated a certain amount of oppositional thinking by painting the world as being gripped in a gnostic struggle between the forces of darkness and the forces of light. In a *New York Times* essay, Tamar Lewin described her three-year-old daughter's fears of witches and ghosts. She then compared these fears to the infamous statement about feminism by evangelist Pat Robertson during the 1992 balloting on an Iowa equal rights amendment. Robertson described the proposed ban on discrimination against women as "not about equal rights for women," but "about a socialist, antifamily political movement that encourages women to leave their husbands, kill their children, practice witchcraft, destroy capitalism and become lesbians" (Lewin 1992, 26). Robertson's remark is a fine illustration of the immature oppositional thinking that is more appropriate to small children than to the religious leadership of the church.

The Fear of Being Dependent

One way in which some men derogate other men is through accusations of being "tied to Momma's apron strings." Some men refer to their wives as "a ball and chain." When I was in seminary, the "thorn in Paul's flesh" was sometimes identified as his wife, implying that to be married inflicted permanent pain. Men's conditioning to value control, independence, competitiveness, and self-gratifying spontaneity leads them to fear dependency as feminine, as a regression in their childhood individuation from their mothers — in short, as a serious threat to their masculine identity. Relationship commitments are not easy for either men or women, in their daily working-out. But for some men, the commitment demanded by a covenanted relationship forms an oppositional bipolarity with their sense of independence. The particular role of Christian ministers in helping men face their dependency fears is as much a theological education task as it is therapeutic, helping men to understand that Christian covenants, including marriage, are commitments of voluntary giving, rather than traps, threats, or potentials for shame.

The Price of Fearing Shame

The price for living as though life and relationships were always one-up-one-down contests is costly. Much of the dysfunction that appears in traditional male behavior can be attributed to the consequences of defensive strategies to avoid losing whatever "face" is measured by inherited gender roles of masculinity.

Being on guard. As in a human pyramid at the circus, staying on top is not easy and demands enormous concentration. In *Couples,* John Updike describes the protagonist as a man always on guard: "the world wore a slippery surface for Piet; he stood on the skin of things in the posture of a man testing newly formed ice, his head cocked for a warning crack, his spine curved to make himself light" (1968, 26). In the military, the more stressful a guard duty is, the shorter the watch. In many men's lives, guard duty against losing face is a permanent state, without respite. The only place men may feel free from this endless alert is at home, but even so, too many marriages have also become an arena for a win-lose competition.

Falling silent. Men's dysfunctional behavior at home then becomes another price exacted by the fear of losing face. When at last a man does not wish to be on guard for a while, he lapses into himself in silence, floating, even without introspection. Conversation studies usually show that men tend to talk in public groups more often than women, and from two to three times longer. At the same time, many ministers report that the most common complaint wives make about their husbands' behavior at home is "He never talks to me!" Tannen (1990, 76–77) addresses this discrepancy by distinguishing "report-talk" from "rapport-talk." Women will employ small talk in order to promote rapport. Most men have no use for this type of connecting talk, having been trained that the primary purpose of conversations is to report information or solve problems. On guard all day at work to make sure they are one-up, imparting information in ways designed to prove their expertise, solving problems in manners calculated to prove their indispensability— when men come home they lapse into exhausted silence. Home is where men relax; for their wives, home may be a lonely place, where they seek rapport but are ignored. What men and women need from their home life together is often different.

Protecting turf. Protecting turf may mean men's guarding their independence, their detachment, and the predictability of their lives, or it may mean protecting something as symbolic as the television remote control (a 1992 poll for *TV Guide* by Peter D. Hart Research Associates revealed that 41 percent of men control the remote in their homes, as opposed to 19 percent of women). To keep track of so many threats—including having one's ball game turned off—coming from so many directions means that each and every detail of men's lives must be kept in careful balance; if one thing gets out of order, the whole house of cards may come crashing down. Men's energy, then, goes into offense and defense instead of connecting and interlocking in relationship. Astrachan tells of a father who felt his daughter had turned against him when her feminist consciousness was raised at college: "I felt like I was walking down an alley and being attacked from the back. I just couldn't understand what it was all about. My God, I'd been breaking my ass all these years, trying to get money to take care of these people, like many other men" (1986, 317). This father had carved out financial security as the turf within which he proved his masculine provider skills. When his daughter challenged him with the idea that providing is a poor substitute for affectionate love, he felt shamed and defensive.

Feeling stressed. A fourth price that men pay for being on guard is the psychological and physical stress that leads to emotional dysfunction. In speaking with men about their fathers, one repeatedly hears stories of angry eruptions that seemed to come without any warning. For some children, baiting Dad until he blows up becomes a variation on Russian roulette, gambling to see which barb or antic will set off the explosion. If men's emotions are already bottled up, and then the extra energy of unbearable stress is added to the mix, the result is an explosion that seems irrational and can become emotionally or verbally violent. Spouses and children approach such men cautiously, finding their unpredictability difficult to live with. For some men, saving face means never having their authority challenged, but defending one's inflated sense of authority from all criticism, however constructive, is an emotionally stressful task. The Christian minister can help men face the price of this fear by working with them to separate issues of authority and control from their fear of being shamed as insufficiently manly.

Telling lies. Men tell lies to cover their powerlessness against more powerful men and their powerlessness against their own shame. They brood about how short they have fallen of their inherited masculine ideal: "The men we carry in our minds . . . and how they differ from the real lives of most men" (Sanders 1991, 76). Lies compensate for the face a man has lost, desperate attempts to convince himself and others that some perceived shame is unfounded and undeserved. Men feel guilty for telling lies, but they feel even worse for the shame that caused them to lie in the first place.

HELPING MEN FACE THEIR FEARS

The predictable result of repeated competition in order to save face and avoid shame is what some have called "cosmic narcissism" combined with a deceptive fragility. Both may be the product of men's repeated efforts to save face. Masculinity, like any artificial social construct, is fragile. The male ego seems so impenetrable because fragile items must be unusually well defended. A wall must be built around a man's perception of what is appropriately masculine and how well he has succeeded in acting out that perception, even if the wall is constructed of lies in order to save face. Masculinity is so fragile that a man fears that when or if his ego crumbles, nothing, no identity, will be found inside.

Listening Behind the Lies

Possibly the most difficult lesson for a minister to face in dealing with men is that men do not always tell the truth. On one level, no one tells the truth, for everyone's perception of reality is skewed by preconceptions and human limitations. Men are prone to telling partial truths constructed to show them as being one-up and to hide their shame. Men cannot help telling lies— exaggerating their toughness and their successes—if they are victims of their own masculinity ideals, the mythic masculine image that we have inherited from the patriarchs. Ministers must presume that they are hearing a partial truth, and respond on the basis of having been given incomplete information.

Every story can be told in more than one way, without any damaging of the truth; at the same time, the truth is bigger than any individual part of it. Indeed, storytelling has become an increasingly accepted technique within the repertoire of skilled ministers. When I was in seminary, my godmother Madeleine L'Engle came to teach creative writing as an elective. Our first assignment was to write a short story. When we turned in our assignment, she then handed it back, saying, "Now rewrite exactly the same story, only this time tell the story from the point of view of a character in the story other than the original narrator." A third time she returned it, saying, "Rewrite it again, from the point of view of still another character in the story." And so we told the same story in so many ways, each time from the point of view of a different character. Although each version remained the same story, each time it sounded quite different because the "truth" was told from the point of view of a different character in the plot.

When listening to a man in crisis tell the history of his marital problems, the minister must remember that the same story could be told in a different way by the man's wife, his mother, his mother-in-law, his children, and his best friend. All stories contain some truth, and all stories are incomplete. Because all stories are true in this sense, all must be treated as true, but the minister's response to what is being told must always include the recognition that the information is true but partial. This simple fact should preclude the minister's jumping to facile conclusions. It should also preclude the minister's offering of advice, for advice offered on the basis of incomplete information runs a high risk of backfiring.

Awareness of the many faces of truth gives the skilled minister a creative means of listening behind the stories that men initially present. A careseeker might be encouraged first to tell his version of a troublesome event, but then to tell it again from another point of view. For example, a husband might tell the story of a marital quarrel from his own perspective. Once some of the emotional interference has been cleared away, he may be encouraged to tell the story of the same quarrel again, but this time from his wife's point of view. In such a way, new insights are gained, emotional misunderstandings and miscommunications are clarified, and the careseeker may find himself better equipped in the future to deal with threatened loss of face. Storytelling feels less threatening to many men than do the more confrontational types of pastoral counseling. Storytelling has also proved effective in premarital counseling and in family counseling that involves parents and young children.

Affirming the Shamed: A Case Study

Betsy made an appointment to speak with a minister about her husband Warren's compulsive gambling. By the time she arrived, Betsy was at an advanced level of despair and agitation. She made wide-ranging accusations about Warren's frequency of gambling and the amounts of money he lost. She even suggested that Warren was embezzling funds from work to support his compulsion. The minister's response to Betsy was caring but cautious, and he requested some time with Warren in order to hear his side of the story.

Having spoken with Warren, the minister was convinced that something was terribly wrong in the couple's marriage, but he was not convinced that Warren was a compulsive gambler, or even that Warren's gambling had reached a level that warranted intervention. The minister suggested regular meetings with both Betsy and Warren to explore underlying issues in their marital relationship. The minister's caution made Betsy feel unsupported, and in her state of alarm, she decided to take her accusations of embezzlement directly to Warren's employer. An investigation was conducted but no evidence of embezzlement could be found. By this time, the resentment between Warren and Betsy had escalated to such a point that Warren filed for divorce.

Warren was telling the truth and not telling the truth. He was playing the weekly lottery, causing an occasional pinch in the family budget but not, in the later opinion of the minister, gambling at a level that could be called addictive or compulsive. To the minister's face, Warren insisted he was not gambling at all.

Betsy too was telling the truth and not telling the truth. Warren was gambling, and something was wrong in their marriage. Not knowing how to name what was really wrong, she grabbed for the most obvious explanation, turning it into an accusation without enough evidence to support her claims. This set of misperceptions, however, is not in itself enough to explain the emotional tension of the relationship or its ultimate dissolution.

Warren was shamed by the way Betsy had made the problem in their marriage public, taking it to a minister and then to his employer without clearing it with him first. To cover his shame, Warren accused Betsy of being mentally unstable and a compulsive liar. Betsy was correct that the marriage was in deep trouble and could not survive without intervention, but she was shamed by the miserable tensions she and Warren felt between them. She blamed the tensions on a convenient cause that did not reflect on her own person — his gambling. Because each had lied out of shame, each had backed the other into a corner. Because neither would concede to having lied out of shame — to admit to lying would have meant loss of face in a situation where neither party was willing to lose anything more to the other — the marriage was not salvageable. The minister never was able to discover the source of the marital problem, for neither Warren nor Betsy was interested in the minister's help after the divorce.

Because the subject of this book is counseling men, Betsy's needs will not be addressed here although she initiated the pastoral contact. Both spouses in this case are in need of skilled care, and a responsible minister would provide Betsy and Warren with the concern and support appropriate to the unique needs of each. What would a minister have to offer a man in crisis like Warren to help him through his shame? Some ministers might be tempted to suggest that Warren go to confession to deal with his shame. The sacramental form of confession bears a marked resemblance to the four-stage process that Carl Jung believed to be foundational to successful therapy — confession, elucidation, education, and transformation — and has for centuries been an effective means of pastoral care within the more liturgically oriented denominations.

Confession might be appropriate in relation to Warren's abusive pattern of gambling, but it would not address the manner in which he had been publicly shamed by his wife's accusations. In his book *Is Human Forgiveness Possible?*, John Patton observes that one can confess and be forgiven for actions or thoughts that one has initiated, or even committed inadvertently, but one cannot find relief by confessing the sins, judgments, or opinions of others. For example, if one loses a job on the basis of rumor and innuendo, or even on the basis of personality conflict, one is shamed in the eyes of a suspicious public. The sacraments of confession and absolution are not designed to deal with such loss of face that results from being caught and exposed, or the loss generated by others' assumptions or ridicule. Yet the shame is felt as deeply as for any heinous transgression for which the church offers reconciliation, and the need for affirmation cannot be ignored.

A man suffering loss of face has no act of omission or commission to confess, but rather may have been shamed by the patriarchy or other outside forces through no fault of his own. An alternative set of stages in the healing process is necessary to rid oneself of shame (Augsburger 1986, 135):

1. Recognizing that one has a goal-oriented image of oneself that has been violated by the shaming.
2. Reclaiming the set of values upon which that self-image has been constructed and which inform the individual's personal goals.
3. Grieving for what has been lost or betrayed, and examining how one's values may actually leave one vulnerable.
4. Reaffirming that ideals are goals to be sought rather than judgments to be dreaded.
5. Recommitting oneself toward rebuilding and regaining respect.

In the case of Warren and Betsy we are dealing with the death of a relationship, and therefore the minister should also watch for the classic stages of grief: denial and isolation, anger, bargaining, depression, and acceptance (Kübler-Ross 1969). In working through grief, the careseeker needs to be affirmed rather than forgiven, confirmed rather than educated. His sense of self (ego) as well as the self he is working toward becoming (ego-ideal), both wounded by the loss of face, need to be supported and healed. As well, he needs to grieve his perceived innocence in victimization, and to examine in the presence of some community why his values have been chosen, challenged, and re-chosen. With the support of the minister, those suffering shame need to be loved into wholeness by their friends and families. Because shame and loss of face are measured in terms of one's public standing, the community bears the opportunity to bless those shamed in their redress.

What the Minister Has to Offer

The minister above was correct in his caution with Betsy, just as he would have been correct to be cautious with Warren. Both Betsy and Warren were telling the truth from their own unique perceptual and emotional capacities, but in both cases that truth was only partial. All of the various stages discussed—Jung's confession, elucidation, education, and transformation; Augsburger's recognition, reclamation, grieving, reaffirmation, and recommitment; and Kübler-Ross's denial and isolation, anger, bargaining, depression, acceptance—are predictable reactions from either Betsy or Warren in the midst of untangling a marriage gone sour. Naming these various emotions and reactions is a critical part of the healing process.

Most situations of shame require extended counseling in order to deal with a shattered ego or ego-ideal and to help identify ways in which the blessing of the community can be sought again. In such cases, the skilled minister will probably find it appropriate to refer a shamed one to more intensive therapy and then to provide the sorts of support that allow that therapy to continue long enough to produce results. In the case of Warren and Betsy, the minister had been consulted too late to save the marriage, but pastoral care for both as individuals would still have been a possibility had either so wished.

Men whose ego has been shattered need healing from shame in addition to whatever confession and forgiveness are appropriate. They need a minister's support in seeking to reclaim four things: their sense of self; their connection between self and the constructive side of the mythic masculinity that sustains them; their sense of continuing connectedness to others; and the courage not to lie anymore. In-depth therapy for these issues may be beyond the minister's training, but the minister retains the capacity to listen, to accept, to support, to love men in crisis, and in the midst of shame, to offer them the welcome and blessing of the community whose Savior cried out, "Those who are well have no need of a physician, but those who are sick" (Matt. 9:12).

3

EMPLOYMENT AND RETIREMENT

Work—whether in an office, a factory, or other setting—is where men spend most of the hours of their day, many more than with wives, lovers, or families. Men derive the proof of their masculine identity from their jobs, for the workplace is the arena where champions are made or broken, where one can prove whether he is tough enough to take it, clever enough to work his way to the top, or mature and reliable enough to be given responsibilities that will make him a model of success.

We live, however, in an age of increasing specialization, automation, and shrinking opportunity. These factors also affect the way in which men work out their identities. One of the most serious threats to masculine identity is the impersonalization found in many of today's highly technical jobs. In the past, a man's work was a critical determinant of his identity as a manly man, and men were trained to explain who they were by giving the title of their employment position. Boys were taught to explain the mythical stature of their fathers by naming the parents' role at work. Today many jobs provide little or no meaning in the way of identity to the person who performs them. "I am an electroencephalograph technician" means nothing to most people (Doyle 1989, 176), nor does "I am an auto assembly-line worker."

MASCULINITY ON TRIAL

As jobs become more meaningless, power is increasingly concentrated in the hands of the few. It is these few whom we term the patriarchs. In our society, they are still primarily powerful white middle- and upper-middle-class males, although some women have been allowed or have chosen also to join the ranks of the powerful, abusive people. Men find that they must be particularly wary of the patriarchs, those who aspire to join the ranks of the patriarchs, and those whose own masculine identity is so shaky that they must prove it constantly by hurting other men who threaten to compete. Along the way, many men develop a victim's mentality and the tendency never to let down their guard for fear of sudden attack from unexpected quarters.

The vast majority of people—female and male—in our society remains powerless and psychologically if not socially and economically disenfran-

35

chised. Most powerful institutions such as parliaments and business corpora-
tions are male-dominated. The powerful do not need to be relationship-
healthy; they need only to protect their power (Hopcke 1990, 54). An
important dynamic in the psychological dis-health of patriarchy is the
amount of sexual sublimation that clubs of powerful men must exercise in
order to keep them bonded enough so that they do not consume each other.
Aggression and competition must be carefully circumscribed by elaborate
rules and conventions. The games that patriarchs play with each other, including the sexual games that occur naturally between any two human
beings, must be channeled into narrow patterns of acceptable dress, behavior,
conversation, reaction, and negotiation.

One of the powers exercised by patriarchy is self-perpetuation, the power
to hand-pick the next generation of patriarchs. This dynamic has been explored by controversial sociologist Lionel Tiger in his book *Men in Groups*
(1969). Tiger draws a powerful analogy, claiming that the way men select
their workmates and professional peers is no different from the way in which
they select sexual partners. The bonds that patriarchs establish among themselves generate emotional and personal satisfaction and are designed to make
the patriarchs look good, just as they have chosen spouses to make them look
good. These patriarchal bonds are constructed to bind people together in a
division of labor that makes them dependent on one another and that guards
the bonding process as so inherently gender-specific that the inclusion of
women is not appropriate. Tiger's explanation sheds light on why patriarchy
seems so impervious to advocates of equality and justice and so quick to
punish—with a wrath comparable to sexual rage—those who challenge it. In
patriarchy, men are so determined to protect their own privilege and entitlement that they will bond together to defend it no matter how much violence
the defense creates or how many fall victim to the distortion of God's image
through abusive forms of mythical masculinity.

THE DYNAMICS OF POWERLESSNESS

One reason that men are trapped in positions that make them vulnerable to
patriarchal abuse and paternalism is the virtually unchallengeable assumption
that in a society where traditional marriage is still the norm (in spite of the
nuclear family being the most rapidly shrinking part of our population), men
must work. Men view women as having three options: full-time employment,
full-time domestic responsibilities at home, or some combination of employment and domestic life. Yet they view themselves as having only the options
of full-time employment, full-time employment, or full-time employment
(Farrell 1991, 83). Men are hooked into this limited choice by their need to
prove their masculinity over and again with no other accepted arena in which
to work out their masculinity, and by the inherited myths that males are "ordained" to be procreators, protectors, and providers.

Some part of men's reaction to the women's movement is shaped by wom-
en's accusation that all men are powerful. Although they may not easily admit

it, most American men perceive themselves to be quite powerless and are upset and angered by women's accusations. At a deep level, they want to say to women: "Don't call me powerful, because I don't want to be blamed for the way things are, and besides I really don't have the power you think I do. On the other hand, don't call me powerless, because that's not who I'm supposed to be." Men are trapped in this Catch-22. Andrew Kimbrell states it this way:

> While recognizing the pervasive victimization of women, we must resist the view of some feminists that maleness itself, and not the current systems of social control and production, is primarily responsible for the exploitation of women. For men who are sensitive to feminist thinking, this view of masculinity creates a confusing and debilitating double bind: We view ourselves as oppressors yet experience victimization on the personal and social level. (1991, 70)

No measure of wealth or power can fill the emotional void that men feel in the face of this powerlessness. This claim of powerlessness is often difficult for women to hear; relatively speaking, men as a group do have more power than women. But men's power is not as comprehensive as many women assume. The private experience and feelings of individual men may well not match women's hard-earned perceptions that males are automatically powerful by right of gender. The fact is that men's unsettling assumption of categorical power is underscored regularly by their feelings of powerlessness in the one arena in which society teaches them to prove their manhood.

THE HOME TOLL OF JOB STRESS

Most men are raised not simply to compete, but to win at all costs. Men now in their forties, for example, were taught as children to venerate the example of two particular patron saints. The first is football coach Vince Lombardi, quoted as saying that "Winning isn't everything; it's the only thing." The second is the Lone Ranger, who always kept secret his true identity. Placing such a high premium on winning, combined with never being allowed to reveal one's self as either human or vulnerable, produces the stress under which most men work. Georgia Witkin-Lanoil describes these people as Type A personalities. Subsequently that classification as a predictor of heart attacks has fallen into disuse; nonetheless, it describes some men's feelings in the workplace:

> Certain types of personality say: "I am never satisfied with my achievements; I am impatient with myself, and others (but try to hide it); I am not sure that I can control my family's feelings, so work becomes my world; I have "status insecurity," so work becomes my world; I am not sure I am really lovable, so work becomes my world." (1986, 157–58)

James Doyle puts it differently: a man must constantly be on his guard, as he never knows when the guy next to him will yell, "Race you to the corner!" (1989, 172).

Harming Self and Others

The three classic effects of job stress are absenteeism, accidents, and alcoholism. Ironically, all three are ways in which men do harm to themselves because they do not know how to address the problems of the workplace upon which their selfhood has become so dependent. They become not only victims of the patriarchy but victims of themselves. Witkin-Lanoil presents us with an additional way in which males respond to stress, which she terms "John Henryism." The legendary black railroad worker vowed that "Before I let that steam drill whip me, I'll die with a hammer in my hand." As we know, John Henry beat the steam engine, and promptly fell over dead. "The John Henry response to stress . . . is a way of controlling stress through determination and hard work" (Witkin-Lanoil 1986, 153–54). This common response, particularly among executives, too often leads to the same terminal results that befell John Henry.

Job stress continues to appear primarily as a problem suffered by males, even though vast numbers of females have entered the workforce. (Women seem to have a different set of responses to job stress, including depression and eating disorders.) Changing times have begun to demand that men be more involved in the maintenance of the household, including child care and grocery shopping. Yet the burden of these nurturing responsibilities continues to fall on the shoulders of women while men continue to exhibit the classic symptoms of job stress. What prevents men from opting to devote more time to nurturing and less to their strenuous but unrewarding and powerless jobs, the sort of choice that many women have already made?

Women, who classically have been enculturated to value relationships more than job success as a source of identity affirmation, may find their sense of pride diminished by concentrating less on their jobs, but do not find their sense of femininity diminished. Men, who classically have been enculturated to devalue relationships and to value job performance, find that a reduced concentration on their success at the workplace means less opportunity to prove their masculinity and exert their independence. For many men, increased commitment to the maintenance of family life is frightening. It makes them worry that their male peers, whose approval they depend on to affirm their masculinity, will find them less manly, for our changing times have not yet found a way to affirm nurturance as an appropriate expression of manhood.

What the Minister Has to Offer

A minister can suggest constructive ways of dealing with job stress. For a man in crisis over the pressures of work (and for his family), the following suggestions may be helpful:

1. Encourage his participation in stress burn-off techniques, including physical and emotional outlets. Many men put their own emotional and physical health low on their priority list, for the simple reason that they are not trained to nurture anyone, including themselves. After proper advice from a doctor, increasing a regimen of exercise will provide greater emotional

stability as well as enhance physical well-being. Men should also be encouraged to look for regular opportunities to laugh together with their families and friends.

2. Encourage a rest period after work stress. Almost all men (and almost all women!) need some sort of transition assistance between the workplace or commuter traffic and home. Spending twenty minutes alone when one first comes home from work is as effective as a cocktail, and if the situation is structured so that the spouse's needs are also met, is much less injurious to health and relationships.

3. Encourage him to talk to someone other than his spouse or partner. This is not always easy to do because of men's resistance to talking over their work problems, especially with their families. Some men may wish to talk to a physician or a minister. Or they may welcome involvement in a men's group, where in the course of a trusting, less emotionally loaded environment, they can talk about stresses and feelings they are reluctant to discuss within their families.

WORKING ALONGSIDE WOMEN

A man's place in the workforce is often precarious. He may have sacrificed some of his personal need for masculine affirmation in order simply to be left alone to do his job. The entrance of women into the workplace is perceived as threatening both men's power and other men's uneasy compromises with power.

With a limited emotional repertoire and little experience in processing emotions in a constructive way, some men know no other way to respond to threat than with anger and emotional abuse. Men's ordinary banter at work is an unconsciously negotiated balance between bonding camaraderie and competition veiled by jocular threats. The entrance of women into the workplace jeopardizes this balance and ultimately forces changes. Not knowing how to behave or what the new rules are expected to be, some men greet these women with covert resistance or even outright hostility. Astrachan analyzes these emotions as an expression of sex-role strain (1986, 28).

At the same time, most men have bought into patriarchy's definitions of who is worthy of dignity and respect and who is not, and all the stereotypes of the other gender passed down through generations of inherited assumptions about masculinity and femininity. As a male manager remarked during a famous study by business sociologists Anne Harlan and Carol Weiss, "Most men just don't like reporting to women because a woman's a woman. It's an insult to their intelligence" (Astrachan 1986, 151). However much one is tempted to question that manager's intelligence, his remark does convey an attitude that women entering the workforce have encountered repeatedly.

Certain men not only have trouble taking orders from women or working with them collegially, but cannot even listen to women. Linguistic researchers such as Deborah Tannen have discovered that in conversation patterns, men listen to women less frequently than women listen to men, because the act of listening has different meanings for each of them. Some men really do not want to listen at length, either to a man or to a woman, because they feel doing so frames them as subordinate (Tannen 1990, 143). If men are trained to assume that social intercourse is always a one-up-one-down competition, then being a listener as opposed to a teller must be a position of disadvantage, to be rejected as inappropriate to masculine behavior.

Patterns of Sexism

The issue of women in the workplace is not necessarily as simple as the competitiveness men assume as a given within human relationships. There is a sexism inherent in most men's patterns of talking and listening, for while these men do not like to listen to either men or women, they still listen to men more often than to women. They will correct, contradict, and interrupt women much more often than they will other men. Some have tried to explain this as evidence for men's devaluation of women. In *How Men Feel*, Anthony Astrachan puts forth a disturbing explanation for the sexism that is still pervasive in the workplace: Men fear women because they do not comprehend how to reconcile female competence and female sexuality (1986, 150).

Astrachan continues his analysis by pointing out how frightened men are by women's skills at verbalization. Something so basic as women's great facility at human communication registers with some men as a threat, particularly in the workplace where men's interactions with one another are so carefully controlled.

> And [men] see all kinds of threats. If you go to parties, most business types sit around going "Glug, argh"; they're extremely nonverbal. Most of their wives, and most of their female colleagues, are much more verbal. I think that frightens them, the notion that all that communicating energy might suddenly explode and be used in ways other than arranging social functions. There are a million threats that surround men all the time. (1986, 151)

A million threats include masculinity daily on trial; the power of patriarchy; the stress of having to win yet never letting anyone know one's true identity. Add to these the threat men perceive that women will displace them in the workforce so that men will no longer be able to fulfill their "natural" function as providers. Add further the sexism inherent in gender-role stereotypes in which many men have been trained from childhood, and one has the explosive mixture that results in the pernicious practice of sexual harassment in the workplace.

Sexual Harassment

The Clarence Thomas–Anita Hill hearings brought the issue of sexual harassment into the light of public concern. Of course women sometimes sexually harass men; men have even won lawsuits against women for harassment. Instances of homosexual harassment between subordinates and supervisors are also known. The vast majority of instances of sexual harassment in the workplace, however, continue to be the harassment of women by heterosexual men. It is more common for powerful men to harass subordinate women, but it is not unheard of for a subordinate man to harass his female supervisor.

Men who fear women—and I believe that, down deep, this includes almost every man—must transform women who are professionally competent into some other less powerful role in order to be able to work with them, particularly if those women are in a position of authority. Powerless men are usually unable to transform competent powerful women in actuality, but they are able to transform them within their imaginations. They transform women through jokes, through casual remarks, in their attitudes, and in their fantasies. These fantasies develop out of men's fear of addressing women as they are. The only alternative is to strip these women of power, making them over into something that men believe they know how to handle. It is easy to underrate the competence of a fantasy figure. It is no longer uncomfortable to be challenged by the power of a fantasy; a man simply has to turn off his imagination, and she is destroyed.

The tendency of men to make women into fantasy objects—mother, lover, whore, emasculator—explains why many men do not understand what sexual harassment is and why it is at last off limits. All forms of harassment are actually power plays, the exploitation of the less powerful by the more powerful. This implies, at first glance, that these men consider themselves superior to women. On more careful examination, we understand these power plays to be desperate attempts to mask men's powerlessness. This explanation helps us understand why harassment is so difficult to root out of the workplace, and why we still have a long way to go in the raising of men's consciousness. Those who are frightened by their own powerlessness will not be easily convinced. For them harassment is a survival issue.

SUPPORTING MEN WHO HAVE BEEN FIRED

The ultimate proof of powerlessness is losing one's job. If a man's identity is derived almost exclusively from his position in his place of employment, then to lose his job is a quadruple catastrophe: loss of income, loss of structure to his day, loss of purpose, and at a foundational level, loss of masculine identity or "face." This quadruple whammy explains why men are so devastated by the loss of their jobs, and why the more powerful a man has imagined himself to be in the workplace, the more exaggerated the effect of his being let go. A minister will find his or her skills challenged to the extreme in dealing with the unemployed.

Breaking Down Isolation

Unemployed men are likely to become isolated, to shut themselves in their homes, even to shut themselves away from family and friends, for they feel shamed. Gloria Emerson describes the networking by which women approach unemployment, and the contrasting isolation typical to men. Men, too, had friends, but often the other men were likewise out of work. Men could not manage the effort to see those who were still on the job, and they

dreaded seeing men who were unemployed like themselves. It was simpler to
stay alone; they knew a self-distrust as their lives began a deadly shrinkage.
For male friends who were accustomed to doing things together—hunting
or fishing or other diversions—their activities required planning and cost
money. Now even a beer in a bar cost too much for the men whose lives had
come down to the counting of coins. Most of the men had wives, but their
wives were not their friends; they were something else altogether and knew
too much to be a diversion or a fresh source of consolation. They were wit-
nesses to the disaster, women watching (1985, 159).

The almost unbearable loneliness, pain, and shame these men carry make
them a challenge for the minister. Certainly these are among the oppressed
and cast down, those who are suffering and heavy burdened, to whom the
minister is commanded by Christ to reach out, to offer a cup of water and a
constantly supportive presence. These men feel alone, isolated, unwanted, in
pain, confused by what went wrong. Above all, they have been shaken to the
core of their masculine identity. Charles and Wayne Oates remind ministers
to begin their support of unemployed men with the promises of Christ, echo-
ing Matthew 25: those in pain are the suffering beloved of God (1985, 19).
Reassuring words in themselves, however, are not enough to sustain unemployed men in the hourliness of their crisis.

What the Minister Has to Offer

Those who have a ministry to the unemployed speak enthusiastically of the
value of forming support groups designed specifically for the mutual care of
jobless men. Such damaged men, more aware of their powerlessness than
ever, are reluctant to spend time with friends who are still employed, those
who still have structure and purpose in their lives. Long daytime hours, when
former friends are at work, throw the unemployed together but, without some
sense of structure and intentional rehabilitation, the hours are often lost to poker
and drinking and hanging out. Twice-weekly group meetings during the daytime have proved extremely effective. Often men's groups are leaderless, but experts in the care of the unemployed suggest that support groups for jobless men
usually need an official facilitator to help men break through their blockage at
talking to other men about failure and to keep the support group focused on its
purpose. Those who find their ministry in this area should consider seeking special training in the psychology of the unemployed, in the effects of shock and
depression, in suicide prevention, and the appropriate skills of group facilitation.

ADJUSTING TO RETIREMENT

Retirement is uncomfortably similar to the situation of those who have lost
their jobs. Retired men too find themselves suffering from a loss of income,
loss of structure to their day, loss of purpose, and loss of masculine identity.
For these reasons, the incidence of men who die within a year after retirement
is disproportionately high.

Men in retirement, at last having time to face themselves and assess what they have accomplished, may discover that they have become someone they did not wish to be. They may discover that in devoting so much energy and attention to the workplace that has nourished and shaped their identity as males, they have sacrificed most of their intimacy with their spouses and children. Thus for some men, retirement can carry the additional burden of deep regret for the choices made in middle age.

On the other hand, retirement may bring a release from the pressures of having always to succeed while hiding one's true self. This may take the form of a real mellowing by older men, a relaxation not only of pressures but also of strictures, so that men become gradually but naturally more in touch with their emotions, more able to give and receive love, and more open to new ideas. Many people notice that their fathers in old age are more free to shed tears or to be openly affectionate with small children. For these more mature men, the inherited prisons of gender-role expectations seem more forgiving, more open to creative reinterpretation.

What the Minister Has to Offer

Ministers dealing with men who have retired may find the following suggestions helpful.

Structure. Men need to be helped and supported in planning ways to restructure their daily self-care once they can no longer rely on the external structures imposed by the routine of the workplace. Senior men need a deliberate program of physical exercise appropriate to their health condition. They also need to establish other purposive patterns and routines. Too many men attempt to maintain a routine simply for the sake of having one, but purposeless routines quickly become hollow and meaningless. At the same time that senior men need new disciplines, they also need to be encouraged to be gentle with themselves and to explore their natural playfulness and creativity. For perhaps the first time in their lives, they have space to pursue spontaneous interests and to find new ways to care for themselves. As well, ministers should check the sexual education of senior men; many do not understand that the natural aging process of the human body does not have to inhibit sexual expression, although it usually alters familiar patterns of sexual intercourse.

Purpose. If retired men redirect their energies and talents into new professions, vocations, or hobbies, they will retain a sense of purpose and meaning to their lives. A man who retires in his mid-sixties can expect to live another fifteen years; these can be productive, fruitful years in which he chooses to contribute his talents and life-experience to social agencies and volunteer organizations so in need of help. With their mellowing, some men find themselves less afraid to assume what they may previously have considered "women's" jobs, such as volunteering in a hospital or serving on altar guilds in their local parish. Some retirement consultants even suggest that with fifteen years of productive life left, men consider uprooting themselves and learning about life in a different part of the country, or even serving overseas.

These experts would recommend that retired men, while they are still vital, "sell the house, give away the dog, pack a suitcase," and try living out some of the missionary fantasies they have long held hidden.

Perspective. From family systems theory we learn that men need a heightened sensitivity to the way in which their retirement will affect other members of their families. Being home all day may be seen as an invasion of the turf that has been the exclusive domain of those wives who have chosen to spend most of their lives as full-time homemakers. Neither spouse is used to answering to the other all day nor having to check in with someone to coordinate plans. Men are seldom used to the daily chores of grocery shopping and meal preparation and housekeeping; on the other hand, their well-intended efforts to chip in may not be welcomed. As senior men sort through their masculine identity once again, they need to be encouraged to remain aware of how their own changes are creating changes in the lives of others.

Intimacy. A man's intimate marital relationship has probably been structured for most of his life on the assumption that because he is away ten hours a day, he can let slide some parts of his relationship with his wife. Suddenly at home more, he may discover that relationship dysfunctions he has been comfortable ignoring are now placed under a magnifying glass. Perceived faults in his wife, tolerable up to now, suddenly seem more annoying; unhealthy but comfortable patterns of projective identification seem not to work anymore, and he may become resentful or feel trapped. It is not inappropriate for a minister to suggest that a husband and wife adjusting to retirement enter into a brief period of couples counseling to ease these various new strains. As well, learning to share routine housekeeping chores in retirement may give both husband and wife more space to enjoy the relational rewards that are the fruits of their deep familiarity with each other.

Friendship. Finally, senior men need to be supported in their efforts to make new friends. After so many years of professional absorption, they at last have time to laugh and play with their peers, free from suspicion and one-upmanship. Again, a commitment to a regular men's group will provide the senior man a place to explore these new potentials within his masculine identity in the company of others who are experiencing the same changes. Relaxed together in their later life, these men may discover abilities to enjoy each other in intimate friendships that they have never before experienced.

GOD'S PROMISES AND THE WORKPLACE PRISON

Most men spend one-third or more of their lives at some sort of workplace. There, working through their identity in an atmosphere charged with tension and danger, they learn to be self-destructive, to tolerate or foster unhealthy relationships, to fear women and other men. Most men, even if they enjoy their work, feel trapped by the demand that they work at all, for it is not an issue of choice. Many men work in an atmosphere where they have few or no rewards, where they cannot take pride in naming their profession, where they are an anonymous part of a vast machine, where even their best efforts make little difference or positive contribution. For these men, work is a prison, and the older they become the more trapped they feel. One writer on men's experience observes:

> When you have experienced success, you find out that it is a failure experience, it is binding, it is enslaving. Someone else is living your life. Another standard, another image, is defining your life. It is the male image — the image of masculine success. You are living that image; you are not living you. This is bondage. Freedom comes only when you begin living your life. (Doyle 1989, 181)

If success is bondage, then freedom must mean liberation from the imprisoning demands and expectations that the workplace imposes on masculine identity.

God's promises in Isaiah, that prisoners will be set free from their chains, carries little meaning for many men until they can see how applicable the promises are to their work situations. Men need liberation from the oppression and abuses of patriarchy, but they also need liberation from their own drives to compete and from the inherited stereotype that masculinity equals professional success. Even if this liberation is only attitudinal, it is a giant step toward creating a new masculine identity that supports and feeds a man's own health and creates the opportunity for collegiality and partnership with other men and women.

4

BEING PARENTED, BEING A PARENT

Late in life, therapist Carl Jung agreed to talk candidly about his experiences growing up. His father was an ordained minister who eventually became so depressed and disillusioned that he left the ministry; his mother was an emotionally strong woman, although for periods of her life she was physically ill. Confused by her husband, she struck out verbally at her children in the course of disciplining them. Jung poignantly describes an early formative memory that left him both suspicious of women and disillusioned with his father. At this time, Jung was just under four years old.

> I am restive, feverish, unable to sleep. My father carries me in his arms, paces up and down, singing his old student songs. I particularly remember one I was especially fond of and which always used to soothe me, *"Alles schweige, jeder neige . . . "* The beginning went something like that. To this day I can remember my father's voice, singing over me in the stillness of the night. . . . I was suffering, so my mother told me afterward, from general eczema. Dim intimations of trouble in my parents' marriage hovered around me. My illness, in 1878, must have been connected with a temporary separation of my parents. My mother spent several months in a hospital in Basel, and presumably her illness had something to do with the difficulty in the marriage. An aunt of mine, who was a spinster and some twenty years older than my mother, took care of me. I was deeply troubled by my mother's being away. From then on, I always felt mistrustful when the word "love" was spoken. The feeling I associated with "woman" was for a long time that of innate unreliability. "Father," on the other hand, meant reliability and — powerlessness. That is the handicap I started off with. (1973, 8)

Jung did not speak more clearly of how these events led him to such suspicion and disillusionment, but he was obviously more affected by his mother's disappearance into illness and his father's inability to step in as the responsible parent than he was by his father's lullabies or his aunt's generosity.

Jung's father was not a cruel man, perhaps not even powerless in the manner the young boy perceived, but his life history strongly suggests a constant struggle with emotional illness in the form of chronic depression. His father belittled Jung's efforts to reach out to him, particularly to nurse his father's crumbling faith. In the end, Jung's father did prove powerless to keep his faith alive as an ordained minister. Jung portrays his father as rejecting Christianity's sense of grace, purposefully deadening his mind, and refusing to test his faith against life experience. Over and over the two struggled, the father rejecting the son's help, the son deeply hurt by the rejection. Jung writes: "I did sometimes attempt to talk seriously with my father, but encountered an impatience and anxious defensiveness which puzzled me. Not until several years later did I come to understand that my poor father did not dare to think, because he was consumed by inward doubts. He was taking refuge from himself and therefore insisted on blind faith" (1973, 73). Perhaps this event from his family of origin influenced Jung to turn his back on normative Christologies, developing instead a faith riddled with Gnosticism and alchemy. It surely also warped his view of the relations between men and women, and his functioning later as a father to his own daughters.

FAMILY SYSTEMS THEORY

A revolution in the field of pastoral care took place some ten years ago with the publication of Edwin Friedman's *Generation to Generation: Family Process in Church and Synagogue*. Friedman's gift was to make available to pastoral ministers the insights of family systems theory, particularly the work of Murray Bowen. Older patterns of pastoral counseling tended to view the careseeker as an isolated individual in need of help, the minister as the spiritual expert with the answers to the careseeker's problem. This traditional model of caregiving made the minister an authority and the careseeker a supplicant—a model of authoritarianism guaranteed to infantilize the careseeker. Incredibly, this older model ignored the fact that every human being is the product of some sort of family and lives in some sort of family, however loosely defined. None of us leads a context-free existence, and because we are all constantly responsive to both our past and present contexts, counseling must take into account the entire system and not simply the isolated individual.

Murray Bowen, Edwin Friedman, and others have laid out a number of foundational principles to describe the workings of family systems. Summarized as simply as possible, family systems theory holds that systems are composed of a series of interlocking triangles. Triangles may consist of three people, or two people and one idea or memory, or one person and two ideas or memories. Triangles interlock with each other in a complex structure like the diagrams of molecular structures that children study in school, and this interlocking creates a stabile, or homeostasis. Homeostasis is a purely descriptive term, not a value term; it describes the stability but does not judge whether the homeostasis is positive and supportive of the individuals within the balanced system, or negative and destructive (a system can be "balanced off-balance"). That judgment is left to the system's participants, although often they need the assistance of a minister in order to gain the perspective to judge accurately. When those in a system are sick, the system itself becomes infected so that other members of the system get pulled into the sickness. The only way for a careseeker to opt out of a system is to break the power of at least one of the triangles that is imprisoning him or her.

Family Triangles

In *Intimate Partners,* therapist Maggie Scarf describes the way emotional triangles work and why people are driven to commit themselves to or entrap themselves in triangulated relationships, usually with other people, but at times with institutions or expectations or memories. Not all triangles are negative in character, although Scarf and other therapists tend to focus on triangles that produce dysfunction.

An emotional triangle is a repetitive interaction that involves three people. Triangles develop when two people share a problem they cannot talk about (much less resolve); they seek to divert the focus of their attention onto something outside their own tense relationship. Involving a third party (a lover, a child, an in-law, or even a minister) offers a means of deflecting or lowering the intensity of the primary conflict.

Emotional triangles come into being because they offer a disaffected and distressed couple a way of not confronting the problems and disappointments that one or both of them are too scared to talk about openly. When the conflict is enlarged to involve three people, the tensions in the relationship can often be successfully obscured. Getting into a triangle inevitably commits the pair to a series of endless skirmishes, but it helps them stave off the all-out battle that might well end in the destruction of the emotional system itself (Scarf 1987, 141).

Among married couples the most common triangle consists of both spouses and a child or a parent. Ordained persons are familiar with the triangle of minister, spouse, and the demands of the church. Single persons may be triangulated with one living parent and the memory of a dead parent, or perhaps with a suitor and an unhealthy ideal of what a committed relationship looks like. Another triangle with which many men struggle is that of the man himself, his father, and the "mythic father," an abstract socially inherited idea of perfection, a prototype against which the man measures the successes (and more often the failures) of his real father. Some men become paralyzed in their abilities to be a father themselves because they resent their own father's failure to live up to the myth. Whatever abilities they may have had to be nurturers in a healthy relationship are swallowed up in bitterness and disappointment at what they were denied. Ironically, these men frequently visit the effects of this negative triangle on their own children.

Triangulation offers an advantage to people in crisis by allowing them to shift the focus away from the specific problem. When anxiety arises between a couple, they ordinarily have only two choices: to resolve the issue through confrontation of the relational dilemma or to leave the relationship. Because a large part of any person's identity is determined by the relationships he or she lives in, neither the discomfort of confrontation nor the finality of leaving is an immediately attractive option. Therefore, many people tend to find a third person or object that both can focus on and thus avoid having to focus on their relationship. A husband and wife who fear facing their relationship issues can instead focus on an in-law, a misbehaving child, or even a disease or an addictive behavior (as in the case of Warren and Betsy's focus on his assumed gambling), shifting blame and anxiety and thus hoping to avoid a head-on clash between them.

Advice to the Minister

Ministers should approach triangles with caution. First of all, these relationships are exceedingly complex; an exercise in diagramming the many triangles that any one person is caught in will prove the point. Second, the minister needs to remain wary that he or she does not become a third point in a new triangle—the stage upon which two careseekers act out their tensions and conflicts, bonding the two further into their dysfunction, and placing all the tensions upon the shoulders of the minister. Third, the minister should be aware that the person blamed is probably not the real problem, but the scapegoat for a set of problems located elsewhere. In technical terms the person blamed is called the *presenting problem* or the *identified patient*. To illustrate: In his case records, Jung described a young woman who was referred to him for help because of her lesbianism. After extensive counseling, Jung concluded that the young woman's problem was not her lesbianism; she was actually fairly accepting of her lesbian orientation. The problem, said Jung, was the narcissistic mother; the mother was referred for psychiatric treatment while the daughter was dismissed from further counseling (Hopcke 1991, 32).

The identified patient or the presenting problem is what the minister is usually given to work with at first. Only extensive conversation will reveal whether the problem that precipitated the careseeker's crisis is the problem most needing treatment. In any case, it is probable that the careseeker will need the minister's support in breaking out of whatever triangles have imprisoned him or her. Breaking out of triangles is not easy; it produces the same wild and crazy effect as a hurricane striking a giant mobile, sending pieces flying wildly in all directions and banging into each other. Homeostatic systems resist this sort of change and will exert great pressure to force the component parts back to homeostasis, even when the system is itself sick or destructive. Careseekers may crumble under this sort of pressure, sometimes because of unresolved issues from their own families of origin.

FAMILY AS AN EMOTIONAL SYSTEM

No human being has avoided being shaped by a family context at the deepest levels of identity. All families are intensely emotional systems, even those whose interaction exhibits no overt emotion. Our families shape our values and assumptions for us, before we are old enough to make up our own minds. Because these families are the only context we know intimately for the first several years of our lives, we quickly come to assume that what we see in our own families is "normal," the way things ought to be in every family.

We also learn rules and expectations about the behavior appropriate to each gender and we take this information for granted. We incorporate this information as describing "normal" behavior between men and women. We carry it with us as we mature and enter new relationship systems. For the rest of our lives, the ways in which we relate to each other as men and women are shaped by the assumptions and ideas of masculinity and femininity formulated in the families in which we grew up. In that context, we learn the most basic identity lessons: "This is what a man is, and what he does." "This is what a woman is, and what she does."

Everyone, even an orphan, has some family-of-origin context, is shaped by that context, and spends the rest of his or her life either imitating or reacting against it. A child growing up in a family headed by a single mother is shaped as much by the father's absence as by the mother's presence, in terms of the basic lessons of who adult men and women are. Although few people these days grow up in a nuclear family, even the nuclear family is rarely free from dysfunctional lessons at home. A child growing up in a nuclear home may learn that normal families never quarrel, never hug, and never discuss sex. An adopted child may learn that birth parents are supposed to abandon their children. A child of divorce may learn the lesson that adult men are expected to leave their families. Children who grow up in sexually or emotionally abusive families believe that all families operate in that manner and that abuse is an integral part of family life. The power of these patterns in determining our future behavior can never be overestimated.

Changing Images of the Family

We are at a crisis point in our society's understanding of the family. We no longer know whether to praise the family or to condemn it. Even children in single-parent families grow up with an image that the "normal" family is like the Cleavers of "Leave It to Beaver," or like Ozzie and Harriet Nelson's family—or perhaps like the Bunkers of "All in the Family"—although emotionally abused, the Bunkers remained together. But even as our children continue to dream these dreams, statistics show that families with two parents and resident children constitute only one-quarter of American society, and each census shows that percentage to be shrinking slowly but steadily as the number of unmarried people rises. These statistics suggest that although we dream dreams of the nuclear family and assert the necessity of "family values," we do not really know how to translate the dream into reality. Our children are growing up fully aware of that disjuncture. To denigrate the family too much creates self-fulfilling prophecies of failure. To praise it too much creates opportunities for unrealistic expectations or embittering disillusionment, and our children mistrust that something unhealthy is being rammed down their throats.

The family is the arena in which children may learn love and affection and nurturance, but it is also the place where 40 to 50 percent of all girls and 20 percent of all boys are sexually abused by a relative or by an adult who is part of the larger network of family friends. The family is both good and destructive. In the family, children see nurturing fathers and alcoholic mothers, unemployed fathers and professionally successful mothers, abusive fathers and long-suffering mothers, self-sacrificing fathers and patient mothers, sullen fathers and hysterical mothers, adults who love each other deeply, and adults who cannot communicate and barely tolerate each other's presence. All of these lessons from our families of origin are patterns that children are destined to repeat in their grown-up relationships unless some sort of therapeutic intervention is sought. Therefore, no minister can ignore the importance, when listening to men, of asking men to explore how their present behavior is a reflection of the lessons they learned in their families of origin about the ways in which men and women relate to each other.

THE GRIP OF THE MYTHIC MASCULINE

Warren Farrell, whose book *Why Men Are the Way They Are* became a national bestseller, asks whether there is an "invisible curriculum" for boys growing up that differs from that of girls. He answers:

> Yes. For girls, "If you want to have your choice among boys, you had better be beautiful." For boys, it's "You had better be handsome and successful." If a boy wants a romantic relationship with a girl he must not only be successful and perform, he must pay and pursue—risk sexual rejection. Girls think of the three Ps—performing, paying, and pursuing—as male power. Boys see the three Ps as what they must do to earn their way to female love and sexuality. They see these not as power, but as compensations for powerlessness. This is the adolescent male's experience of inequality. (1991, 84)

Boys grow up with a mythic image of masculinity that includes the assumption that if they perform, pay, and pursue, they will have achieved adult manhood and will have the power to demand whatever they want from life and from women. From the beginning they realize that these are roles they must master in order to compensate for the powerlessness they sense when they compare themselves with adults or older siblings.

The mythic masculine with which boys struggle feels easily jeopardized, and strong defenses are erected to protect it over the course of time, not only by the boy himself, but as a result of the pressure of other boys and men, and even women, who are a part of the boy's perception of the world. Even in single-mother homes, the role of father is merged with achievement of manhood so that those who struggle to live up to the socially accepted standards of traditional masculinity struggle also with what it means to act as father. Mythic fatherhood becomes a model as divorced from reality and a boy's sensitivity as is mythic masculinity. In order to be a good father, a man must choose to let go of mythic fatherhood.

WHAT KIND OF FATHER WILL I BE?

"When men get together to talk about being men, the first issue is always fathers" (O'Conner 1990, 36). Fathers are men's greatest unresolved issue, if we can trust the conversation patterns repeated over and again by whose to whom we listen. Men want to talk about their fathers, and do so with a sense of pride and often, as well, with a sense of loss and resentment. We appreciate what we know of our fathers but, even more so, we are resentful over what we do not know of them. We know something of what they have done; we know little of who they are, what they valued, and why they too walked around in pain. The first lesson for men is to recognize that their own wounds are the emotional inheritance they received from their wounded fathers.

Father as Teacher

It is not always their fathers from whom men learn the most, but it is their education that men miss the most. Generally what boys know about relating to other people has been learned from their mothers (Erkel 1990, 34). The absence of a father's influence in teaching his children the requisite relationship skills is the product of a marriage model assumed to be traditional—although it is actually a product of the Industrial Revolution two hundred years ago—in which the women took charge of the home and family nurturing, whereas the father went out to provide the income. This strict division of labor has resulted in boy-men who, in the course of growing up, have carved out identities in relation to their female parent but not in relation to their male parent. In the absence of fathers, many lessons go untaught. The effect on children of workaholic or emotionally absent fathers is often little different from the effect of single-mother families.

Yet we also learn some of our most powerful lessons from our fathers: how a man smells, how a man spends his time, what a man is responsible for within the family unit, how a man constructs and defends a public image, how a man reacts to women, how to throw a ball and drive a nail. Each of us longs for his father, wearing his clothes to play dress-up, clomping around the house in his shoes. We use our father's castoffs as talismans, hoping that somehow his masculinity will rub off on us. We pretend to shave in the mirror just like he does. We follow him around the house and the yard, and when we are bigger we accompany him on outings. His is the manhood model we pursue desperately, and most boys reach adolescence before it dawns on them that they do not want to be just like their dad.

Father as Hero

At times, we idolize our fathers too much. In his moving short story "The Kerchief," Shemuel Yosef Agnon describes a young boy's delight as his father returns after several days away from home peddling goods at the local fair:

> Suddenly father bent down, caught me to him, kissed me and asked me what I
> had learnt. Is it likely that father did not know which portion of the week was

being read? But he only asked to try me out. Before I could answer he had caught my brother and sisters, raised them on high and kissed them.

I look about me now to try and find something to which to compare my father when he stood together with his tender children on his return from afar, and I can think of many comparisons, each one finer than the next; yet I can find nothing pleasant enough. But I hope that the love haloing my father of blessed memory may wrap us round whenever we come to embrace our little children, and that joy which possessed us then will be possessed by our children all their lives. (Agnon 1963, 147)

Fathers so raised up are destined either to fall mightily, or to live on in memory as gods divorced from reality, thereby denied the right to be counted among fallible humanity as real persons.

Father as Abuser

Somewhere along the way we begin to learn other lessons from our fathers as well. We learn that men hurt other men. The doctor who delivered us was the first man to hit us, to paddle us to make us cry so that we would suck in our first breath—in rage. When we misbehaved, our mothers said, "Just wait until your father gets home, and then you'll get punished." When we were older she said, "Do you want me to tell your father what you've been doing?," colluding with us so that the powerful man in our family of origin would not hurt us. Our fathers did hurt us when they promised us things and then forgot to deliver, or when they went to work instead of watching us play ball.

Theories of human development keep assuming that fathers are there, actually living in the same house with the rest of the family, performing some useful functions, interacting emotionally with a wife and children, playing a role in his son's life, being a model for the boy. Such blissful days, if they ever existed, have now passed, and fathers wield their influence not by their presence, but by their absence. (Pittman 1990, 50)

Modern society—with the commuter father, weekend father, and even absentee father—leaves young men with less-than-ideal male role models and teachers. Our fathers leave us to make their own fortunes in the public arena, but we are left at home in the private arena, carving out our identities by struggling with our mothers and wondering what happened to Dad's promises that he would be there to teach us. Do young men see their fathers only as people who leave the house early and return late, tired and tense? If they do, then young men will quite likely grow into men who leave the house early and return home late, tired and tense, living for the weekend (Healy 1992, 139).

Father as Boss

Our fathers often model shut-down emotional behavior for us. When we were not sure how to handle a situation as budding young adults, or when we were sorting through options to shape a vision of how men interact with society and the world, we wanted to turn to our fathers for emotional help, for processing, but too often our fathers were as shut down as was Jung's. They had turned those "softer" issues over to our mothers, and so our questions got answered, but in cross-cultural language, a "genderlect" that did not always satisfy our need for our fathers to show us that they loved us as much as our mothers did:

> A German student showed me a card she had received that her mother had covered with handwritten "conversation" inquiring about her daughter's life and health and filling her in on family news. Folded into the card was a brief typewritten note from her father, telling her to go to the university registrar and obtain a form that he needed for tax purposes. (Tannen 1990, 103–4)

In this case, the division had been made: the mother was taking care of the relationship, the father of the business. How often have we seen that men do not write letters, even to their children; they let their wives take care of that. Relationship maintenance cannot be reconciled with being emotionally shut down.

Father as Myth

Ministers should be aware that much of men's conversations actually concern the mythic father and not the real father. In the absence of factual information, the child's imagination kicks in and the child reaches conclusions based on his fears and limited perceptions that may not be congruent with reality. In *Society without the Father*, German psychologist Alexander Mitscherlich theorizes that a child who does not know where his father is during the day will make up an explanation that is limited by the child's immature abilities to conceptualize. Because a child cannot imagine the value of sitting at a desk and rearranging papers all day, he will fantasize that his father is involved in secret espionage, or makes influential government decisions, or is hiding his work because it is illicit or shameful. A son jumps to conclusions because he has not been given information that he knows how to process.

Other men, not knowing their fathers' emotions and fears, come to believe that their fathers did not love them or failed them somehow. These too are the demons of suspicion, doubt, and fear. But in these situations, as in the ignorance of a father's job, it is the mythic masculine that shapes the conclusions we jump to in our imagination, the mythic father whom we seek. Our real fathers are not mythic; they are flesh and blood. They too were "wounded"; they too need our understanding and our forgiveness for their repeated failures, their inability to be as important as they wish we believed—in short, our forgiveness for their being simply human.

We must individuate from our families of origin, from mythic masculinity, and above all from both our real fathers as well as our mythic fathers if we are going to find peace with the men in our history and with our own masculinity. Mature adulthood is not too late to build a sense of independence and choice as an individual in one's own right. Unless the tasks of individuation are accomplished, healthy relationships are a near-impossibility. Because it is within the nature of relationships to change and be fluid, the tasks of individuation need regular attention throughout the stages of adult life—even in maturity as we undergo the natural aging processes of our bodies, our emotions, and our needs. For some this will be more difficult later in life because their fathers are dead and they have no one else with whom to work out their delayed individuation face-to-face. For other men, especially those who are the products of emotionally or sexually abusive families of origin, individuation is easier after the father is dead, when these men are at last free from the tyranny of a warped and violent traditional masculinity.

Mentor as Father

Some men are finding mentors to assist them in their delayed individuation and to work through certain unresolved family-of-origin issues. A mentor is an older man who assumes the role, in relation to a younger man, of guide, teacher, confidant, and father-substitute free from the complications of a blood-father. The mentor's role is to recapitulate the boy-man's experience with his real father, bringing it this time round right, to repair the boy-man's education, to hear those confidences and questions that a man needs to entrust only to another man. To be a mentor is a venerable ancient role whose importance has been too little recognized in recent times. The psychiatric community has joined with the men's movement in recommending that men in their twenties and thirties find mentors to assist them in the search for a healthier profeminist identity (Erkel 1990, 32).

Ministers must approach issues of continuing individuation carefully, especially if they choose to be mentors. While male mentoring has a respected history, it is a complicated role. The temptations of adoration and over-investment in the relationship are a constant threat. Ministers who choose to mentor younger men must realize that mentoring is a transient and artificial relationship, however close. Mentors must be prepared to let go of their careseekers over and over again, no matter how painful, no matter how ill-prepared for independence the careseeker may appear.

PATTERNS GENERATION TO GENERATION

Men who have not individuated properly carry the conflicts from their families of origin into their adult families. We do things, by and large, as we saw them done or in the opposite way as a reaction to what we saw. This tendency to behave in reverse ways is especially evident in emotionally charged situations. Our children may do things opposite from us, and so whatever problems exist within a multigenerational system tend to boomerang from generation to generation (Scarf 1987, 52).

Jung understood this dynamic well. He believed that all tensions that are not resolved in the family of origin are destined to be worked out in the adult male's family. He even recognized this pattern in himself, while working to set up a series of carvings in the garden of his house outside Zurich:

> When I was working on the stone tablets, I became aware of the fateful links between me and my ancestors. I feel very strongly that I am under the influence of things or questions which were left incomplete and unanswered by my par-

ents and grandparents and more distant ancestors. It often seems as if there
were an impersonal karma within a family, which is passed on from parents to
children. It has always seemed to me that I had to answer questions which fate
had posed to my forefathers, and which had not yet been answered, or as if I
had to complete, or perhaps continue, things which previous ages had left un-
finished. It is difficult to determine whether these questions are more of a personal or more of a general (collective) nature. (1973, 233)

Jung was aware of the legacy of "wounded fathers" that can carry down from
generation to generation. A wounded man had a wounded father, the father
was wounded by his father in turn. This wounding is Jung's answer to why
the same problems appear over and over again in generations of father-son
relationships: wounds that are not healed are simply passed down as an emotional inheritance.

One way in which a man may continue identifying with or reacting against
his childhood models of fatherhood is by substituting new persons in the various roles of the dysfunctional triangles he carries with him. If a man was tri-
angled into a negative childhood dynamic with his mother and his brother,
he may, upon leaving home and marrying, simply substitute his wife in place
of his mother in the dysfunctional triangle, perpetuating a dynamic with both
wife and brother that is unhealthy but with which he is familiar enough to be
comfortable. Sometimes the parent within the triangle is invisible, such as a
parent who has died. A father may be deceased, but as long as his memory
continues to dominate the emotional health of his son, the father remains a
powerful point within the primary homeostatic triangles that determine his
son's reactions within relationships.

WHEN A MAN'S FATHER DIES

In October 1896, Sigmund Freud's father died; at the time, Freud was about
forty years old. In "The Interpretation of Dreams," Freud speaks of his father's death as "the most important event, the most poignant loss, of a man's
life" (Gay in Freud 1952, xiii). Carl Jung's tragically depressed father died
when Jung was about twenty-one years old. He too describes the event in
poignant terms:

> The following days were gloomy and painful, and little of them has remained in
> my memory. Once my mother spoke to me or to the surrounding air in her
> "second" voice, and remarked: "He died in time for you." Which appeared to
> mean: "You did not understand each other and he might have become a hin-
> drance to you." . . . The words "[He died in time] for you" hit me terribly hard,
> and I felt that a bit of the old days had now come irrevocably to an end. At the
> same time, a bit of manliness and freedom awoke in me. After my father's death
> I moved into his room, and took his place inside the family. For instance, I had
> to hand out the housekeeping money to my mother every week, because she
> was unable to economize and could not manage money. (1973, 96)

The death of a father foists on a man the role of mythic father, whether he wants it or not, whether he has individuated or not.

Learning to Grieve Openly

As long as a man's father is alive, a secure foundation seems to lie beneath the son, supporting and protecting him as he engages the harshness of the world; another masculinity, no matter how mythic, is there to protect him while he is not yet ready. In chapter 17 of *Women in Love*, novelist D. H. Lawrence describes the feelings of Gerald, one of the two male protagonists, as his father lay dying:

> Meanwhile, as the father drifted more and more out of life, Gerald experienced more and more a sense of exposure. His father after all had stood for the living world to him. Whilst his father lived Gerald was not responsible for the world. But now that his father was passing away, Gerald found himself left exposed and unready before the storm of living, like the mutinous first mate of a ship that has lost his captain, and who sees only a terrible chaos in front of him. He did not inherit an established order and a living idea. The whole unifying idea of mankind seemed to be dying with his father, the centralising force that had held the whole together seemed to collapse with his father, the parts were ready to go asunder in terrible disintegration. Gerald was as if left on board of a ship that was going asunder beneath his feet, he was in charge of a vessel whose timbers were all coming apart. (1975, 213–14)

With the death of his father, the bottom seems to have fallen out of Gerald's world. With the safety net removed, he is now called on to assume the duties of adult manhood, to take his place in the senior generation of authority and responsibility. And he knows that he has not been properly prepared.

What the Minister Has to Offer

In the days and weeks leading up to the death of someone deeply loved, a minister may discover opportunities to teach a man how to mourn. Encounters with a counselee preparing for the loss of his wife or a parent not only provide the minister with the chance to help the man plan practical details of loss—finances, funeral arrangements, the many official forms and certificates—but also provide the chance to rehearse in advance with the counselee how to grieve—the names of the emotions; in what circumstances he will feel safe to grieve; how to move through the lengthy process of grieving in a healthier manner. At a significant level, one is seldom more prepared for a long-anticipated death than for a sudden death. But the days and months marked by protracted illness and suffering give the minister time to rehearse with men the feelings of loss, anger, grief, regret, and denial, and to encourage them to bring to resolution old wounds and memories so that the dying and the mourner can together create what Carl Jung called "a good death," a death of dignity and of peace.

The manner in which the many issues stemming from a man's family of origin are handled determines the course of his relationships for the rest of his life. Ministers cannot afford to ignore the importance of family systems theory in identifying where a man has come from and how the manner in which he was nurtured as a child continues to affect him in adulthood. Our success as parents is to a significant degree determined by the way we were parented. Masculine identity, whether healthy or unhealthy, is a reflection of our childhood experiences, but we work it out as adults in the arenas of marriage, friendship, and the workplace.

5

MARRIAGE AND COMMUNICATION

Whereas men work out their identities as competitor, organizer, and achiever in the workplace, marriage is the stage upon which most men work out their masculine roles as procreator, provider, and protector. Other roles played out within marriage include nurturer, fixer, decider, and teacher. Men are grateful for an opportunity to claim these roles; it gives them purpose in life away from the workplace, providing an opportunity for them to put into play the masculine identity issues that they have struggled with there.

Although marriage in our time is perhaps somewhat less attractive to men than it has been in the past (only about half of the American male population over age sixteen is married), there are many good things to be said about marriage. Those things will not be said here, however, for they are said well in a host of books on the theology and psychology of marriage, materials to which ministers have easy access. Rather, this chapter will concentrate on how men feel in marriage, and how ministers can support men in their struggle to be more relationship-intimate while still maintaining their desired sense of independence.

WHY MEN GET MARRIED

The majority of men marry at some point in their lives. Sometimes these marriages last for decades, but at least half of these marriages end in an average of two years. After a period of being single, most men marry again, and occasionally even a third and fourth time. Our first question then must be, Why is marriage so compelling for men? Four explanations provide possible answers.

Connecting with the Feminine

First, men are conditioned to use women as an outlet for emotions and nurturing tasks that they have been taught by patriarchy to suppress in themselves. Men have emotions, of course, no matter how deeply they repress them, but the expression of emotions is generally considered by society to be the job of women. In order to have an outlet for his own emotions, a man needs to find a woman onto whom he can transfer his emotions so that she will express them for him. The easiest way to find such a woman is to marry

60 COUNSELING MEN

one. The "feminine" or emotional side of men, sometimes referred to in Jungian theory as the *anima,* is usually defined as that part of a man that is concerned with relationships and the voicing of eros, the desire to connect with another. When a man projects half of his personality onto a woman, asking her to tend and vent it for him, the woman is transformed into the competent, all-encompassing, mythic mother, while the man is sentenced to a life of perpetual psychological adolescence as one who has failed to mature into wholeness (Hopcke 1990, 100–101).

This complicated male-female dynamic is not so much an ur-paradigm of the natural order as it is an expression of humanity's desire to sort out inherited gender roles. The original creation stories of most branches of humanity, including that proto-Judaism out of which Christianity sprang, understand humanity as having been created androgynous. The leftover traces of this understanding are found at Genesis 1:27, where the human is pictured as simultaneously male and female. Nor has the subsequent splitting into an irreconcilable maleness and femaleness been without its more regretful modern critics.

Near the beginning of chapter 16 in D. H. Lawrence's *Women in Love,* Rupert Birkin wrestles with the way in which the bifurcation of the human species into genders impedes the emotional maturity of both men and women:

> It was intolerable, this possession at the hands of woman. Always a man must be considered as the broken-off fragment of a woman, and the sex was the still aching scar of the laceration. Man must be added on to a woman, before he had any real place or wholeness. . . .
>
> In the old age, before sex was, we were mixed, each one a mixture. The process of singling into individuality resulted into the great polarisation of sex. The womanly drew to one side, the manly to the other. But the separation was imperfect even then. And so our world-cycle passes. There is now to come the new day, when we are beings each of us, fulfilled in difference. The man is pure man, the woman pure woman, they are perfectly polarised. . . . Each has a single, separate being, with its own laws. The man has his pure freedom, the woman hers. . . . Each admits the different nature in the other. (1975, 192–93)

Attaining Normalcy

A second explanation for men's seeming obsession with marriage is as a guarantee of their normalcy, a reaction that again reflects how tenuous men's sense of their own masculinity may be. Carl Jung was aware of this need for normalcy in himself: "My family and my profession always remained a joyful reality and a guarantee that I also had a normal existence" (1973, 189). Although only half of the men in America are married, marriage remains the standard by which society judges whether a man has reached the fullness of personhood. It is difficult to comprehend the logic by which the married 50 percent of the population can define what is normal for the single 50 percent, but much of this power to define is a holdover from patriarchy's suspicion that if a man's sexuality is not channeled into monogamous wedlock, it will necessarily run amok. Ministers should be sensitive to their own prejudices in

this area and be as equipped to affirm men in their singleness as they are to
support them in working through the issues of marital intimacy.

Avoiding Loneliness

Third, many men seem to fear loneliness. In *Home Alone* the audience cheered
as child actor Macaulay Culkin faced being alone and overcame it with a typical masculine aggressive violence. Ironically, most adult men are driven to an
excessive sense of independence and yet fear what will happen to them if they
achieve it. Many men have what behavioral therapists would term "an ap-
proach-avoidance" response to the subject of time spent alone: they both
desire it and fear it. Men seem to be able to handle independence as long as
they are pushing their way out of intimacy, at the same time fearing being at
home alone, without the busy sounds of wife or children in the next room.

Fathering Children

A fourth reason for men's obsession with marriage is their biological drive to
father children. The perpetuation of oneself through progeny is an outlet for
men's inherent although usually deeply repressed need to nurture and to
teach. For some, procreation is the defense against the loneliness that they
feel within their marriages. Children also seem to be the answer to the loneliness of being old and ignored, of leaving behind no monument, no name
(Isa. 56:5). As well there is the power of prideful curiosity: what will my children be like, and how can I instill in them the values that I have fought so
hard to achieve? This drive to leave behind a marker of their success is one
explanation why homosexual men adopt children, and why heterosexual men
prove their manhood by "making something." (This may also explain why so
many men prefer not to assume responsibility for the use of birth control.)
Because men are biologically unable to get pregnant and give birth, they seek
women who will not only carry their emotions, but carry their children.

COMMON PROBLEMS IN STABLE MARRIAGES

Men, even those whose inability to communicate might suggest otherwise,
commonly have certain expectations of their spouses in the marital relationship. The minister listening to men must be prepared to support male careseekers in working through five common problems men experience in marriage.

Symbiotic Relationships

The process by which men and women create a complicated division of labor
and emotion in a relationship is called *projective identification*. Scarf defines
the phenomenon in this manner:

> Intimate partners often perform this function for one another: experience and
> express what are actually the spouses' unacknowledged and repudiated emo-
> tions. When one person is always angry and the other is never angry, it can be
> presumed that the always angry spouse is carrying the anger for the pair of
> them. And similarly, when one partner is very competent and the other non-

functional (depressed, for example), there is usually an unconscious deal in effect, a collusion about who will take ownership of which particular feelings. (1987, 22–23)

The symbiotic character of projective identification is the result of men's discomfort with their own feelings and women's exaggerated desire for relationship (Letty Pogrebin [1987] has described many women as "relationship-junkies"). Both effects are the obvious product of the dichotomous gender-role stereotypes in which children are trained from the earliest age.

Short-circuited Communication

The most common form of projective identification relationship is one familiar to every experienced minister: the nonexpressive husband and his voluble, highly emotional wife. In this kind of marriage, each spouse has his or her own area of specialization. One partner (usually the woman) carries all of the expressivity, warmth, and feeling in the intimate system, while the other is in charge of cool rationality, attention to detail, and logic. Even for highly successful professional men who manage the business relationships of scores of employees, this counterproductive behavior may describe their home life. In this sense, a man is functional away from home and dysfunctional at home, in that he inhabits a system at home that is infantilizing, emotionally unwhole, and ultimately ungratifying.

Entitlements

Intimacy and autonomy-independence are the polar commodities bartered in a marital relationship. Both partners want both intimacy and autonomy, but as studies show repeatedly, girls are often trained to overvalue intimacy, and boys to overvalue autonomy. Research on young children shows that when girls are playing with girls and a quarrel breaks out, they will find something else to do rather than perpetuate the quarrel and thus threaten their sense of intimacy with each other. When boys are playing with boys and a quarrel breaks out, the boys will often prolong the quarrel, for in so doing they are interacting competitively and aggressively, and by quarreling are defending their autonomy and personal turf. When adult men quarrel with their wives, they are also protecting their turf, although in this case turf means the power to define themselves and their assumed role. As Scarf puts it, the man argues in order to defend his own "ability to say who he was, who she was, and what their relationship was fundamentally all about" (1987, 35). Men's sense of autonomy and entitlement often convinces them that this is a husband's due role in a relationship, but not a wife's.

Boundary Anxiety

Space and boundary issues reflect the condition of a man's ego strength. When facing off with a woman, a man's ego response is shaped by his childhood experiences to register empathy and intimacy as threatening a regression back to maternal dependency. Boys have to work harder than girls to individuate from their mothers, and hence symbolically from all women, so that an invasion of their personal space feels dangerously like the threat of loss of self. The work of Carol Gilligan (1982) and Nancy Chodorow (1978) reveals that from childhood on, men have spaces in their lives that they cannot tolerate having "invaded," by either a man or a woman, and the threat of invasion will at times produce an irrational reaction. Finding space in the midst of intimacy is a difficult task for most men. When pushed to choose between connectedness and control, many men will opt to retain control over their private turf; the damage done to the relationship is a secondary concern.

Mythical Bliss

A final problem experienced by many men within a marital relationship is the struggle to reconcile the myth of marital bliss with the everyday reality of children in diapers, rebellious teenagers, laundry, pots and pans, flu, bills, and in-laws. Men are taught to succeed at what they undertake, to do everything like a project meticulously planned in advance. But marriage and family life are better described as unpredictable and chaotic, with never enough time and energy to accomplish all that needs doing, and marriage is certainly never tidy. As men move more and more into shared patterns of home maintenance and child-rearing, their frustration grows with the realization that life at home cannot be left as neat as one's desk at the office. The days when women alone were competent housewives and men brought home the bacon are gone, but the myth remains. Many men feel that the chaos and unpredictability of daily family life threatens the dignity of their manhood. The tasks of marriage cannot be completed as successfully as building a handsome picnic table or pounding an opponent at racquetball.

MEN AND CONVERSATION

Studies show that men cover more topics more quickly (and at less depth) in a given conversational period than do women and that men tend to communicate *to* others whereas women communicate *with* others. Men have a distinct, more comfortable manner by which they communicate to other men, and a different, less comfortable manner by which they communicate to women. Man to man, conversations tend to be competitive and for the sole purpose of communicating information or imparting opinion. Exchanging details about public news rather than private news has the advantage that it does not make men personally vulnerable. The information they are bartering has nothing to do with them (Tannen 1990, 111).

In his novel *Couples*, John Updike describes Piet's discomfort in conversing with women. Piet is having lunch with his friend Janet, who is having an affair with their mutual friend Harold:

> Janet smiled, tipping a little from her glass into his. "Poor Harold," she said. "He hates indiscreet conversations. It's too female, it threatens him. But you know," she went on, having realized [Piet] would be good to experiment with, "I can't talk to other women comfortably. I could only have said these things to a man." She stated this with an air of having produced a touching confession for

him, but he found it presumptuous and offensive. He thought women should
properly talk with women, and men with men, and that communication between the sexes should be a courtly and dangerous game, with understood
rules, mostly financial, and strict time limits. Ninety minutes was usually quite
good enough, and this lunch lasted longer than that. (1968, 138)

Although Piet's character is portrayed by Updike as sensitively introspective
about the way he physically and emotionally abuses women, Piet still prefers
conversations with rules, imparting information, not probing too deeply.
Janet is not asking Piet for advice, but simply asking him to listen. If the purpose of conversation is either the imparting of knowledge or opinion or the
solving of problems, there is little need to listen, particularly in those marriages where husbands are convinced that they have already heard their wife's
feelings expressed too often.

Conversation as Problem-Solving

All conversations have multiple levels of meaning, the two most obvious
being the message (the actual content of the conversation) and the meta-message (the feel of the conversation, the message conveyed by the context and
the nonverbal signals, in addition to the content itself). Women, in seeking
empathy and affirmation of their feelings, focus more often on the meta-message than do men. In such instances, the point of sharing their concerns and
worries and reactions with a man is not to have the problems go away, but for
the listener to enter into the intimacy of shared response and similar experience. What Tannen calls "troubles talk" is intended to reinforce rapport by
sending the meta-message: "We're the same; you're not alone." When men
focus on the message they are receiving rather than the meta-message,
women feel dismissed, or worse, devalued. Men's advice seems to send the
meta-message "We're not the same. You have the problems; I have the solu-
tions" (Tannen 1990, 52–53). These theories explain why husbands complain that their wives talk too much, while wives complain that their
husbands never listen. Wives are trying to paint a word poem of their feelings, which husbands have never been taught to hear; word poems take more
words than does factual information. And men truly aren't listening to the
meta-message.

Conversation as Competition

In addition to using conversation to convey information or impart opinions,
men use conversation to compete in the one-up-one-down manner they have
learned in order to preserve respect for their traditional masculinity. This is
the accepted explanation why men regularly interrupt each other and, even
more often, interrupt women. If conversations are competitions, then one
plots how to interrupt in order to score a one-up position of superiority or to
adopt a one-down stance of flattery and ingratiation. A common exercise that
ministers assign men is to try listening to a woman complete an exchange of
information or feelings without once interrupting her. Men also use conversation as a form of jocular camaraderie; because they cannot touch or deal

with the discomfort of other forms of intimacy, they resort to hitting on each other verbally. Men also use conversation to draw attention to themselves, but in the midst of a marital quarrel this is not a desired result, so men often simply shut down.

What the Minister Has to Offer

Ministers need to be sensitive to these communication issues to keep them from interfering with the care sought, to turn them to good, and to employ them to point out to men the negative effects of their familiar patterns. Assuming that a female minister can even tolerate listening to men (given women's cumulative awareness that some conversations are but self-aggrandizing monologues), she may find herself regularly interrupted. She should recognize these interruptions as opportunities to work with men in crisis who wish to correct their responses and to cultivate more intentionally the respect and the art of listening.

Male ministers may find themselves caught up in the natural competitive give-and-take of male-male conversation. To succumb to participation in such gamesmanship is tempting to male ministers, for it is the way in which they have been socialized to relate to other men, particularly within the professional sphere. A male minister will need to adopt a posture of subordination and nurturance when listening to men, employing active attending skills in order to subvert the way in which men know how to manipulate other men, including those to whom they have turned for care. The most difficult cases for a minister to deal with are those men who do not wish to talk at all because open conversation about fears and dreams frames these men as subordinate, as supplicants, as not-independent, and therefore, as inadequately masculine.

MEN AND VIOLENCE

Violence in the home—physical, emotional, verbal, or mental—is one of our society's great unsolved epidemics. It is difficult to measure accurately whether such violence is on the increase or is simply being spoken of more openly. Sociological research suggests that violence in the home is on the rise as men feel escalating frustration over their own oppression, women's demands for equality and justice, their children's more open forms of rebellion, a recession economy, and an increasingly judgmental society.

As boys, most males learned to lash out in frustration by using their fists. They did not learn to process their emotions, so the wells of rage that build up in adult men still have a childlike, almost uncontrollable nature once tapped. With a shamefaced wit, Sebastian Junger wrote in the *New York Times Magazine* about hitting a wall out of frustration with his girlfriend, breaking his hand in the process.

> As I went around in my cast, I collected quite a few stories from other people who also punched walls. The majority were men, although I did hear of one woman who beat up a steel fire door. The common theme was that these men

had stored up resentment or anger for years and then something—in my case something so small I hardly remember what it was—made them blow their tops. Given a healthy man's capacity to harm, it's interesting and perhaps admirable how many turned the anger on themselves. I distinctly remember thinking, at the moment of release, Now she'll see how upset I am. Since there apparently aren't any ways for men to show small amounts of pain, my two choices seemed to be either to endure or explode. (1992, 14)

A man's rage and violence within the marital home are acts of desperation as irrational and inappropriate as adulterous affairs. Rage and violence are the product of self-destructive urges misdirected externally. Ultimately it is the man's own ability to process feelings that is deficient, whether due to suppressed emotions, a painful awareness of his powerlessness to control others, lack of communication skills, or unresolved issues from his family of origin. Violence is the attempt to be in charge of whether a relationship will change and grow or remain predictably the same. When understood as an attempt at maximum control, violence displays the ultimate disregard for the wishes and rights of others.

Rage and violence are not only self-destructive; they are assumed at times by men to be a justifiable form of defending one's rights as a male. By exteriorizing his reactions, a man who hits or rapes or abuses emotionally can thereby avoid looking inside himself. Because he does not know how to help himself, he vents his frustration through physical, emotional, verbal, or mental violence. Such a man needs professional help, usually beyond the minister's degree of training.

MEN AND AFFAIRS

Statistically, fifty percent of all married people will have at least one affair during the course of their marriage. The probability is somewhat higher for men than for women, but more recent figures show that gap to be narrowing quickly. A minister must have a clear understanding of the danger that adultery presents to a relationship, as well as how a discovered affair might be turned to the advantage of both husband and wife.

Affairs as Solutions

An affair is a complicated event to untangle, and its impact on a marriage varies according to how widely the affair is known, how long it has gone on, whether it is heterosexual or homosexual, and the degree of commitment made by the adulterer to the third party. In general, ministers should approach the responsibility of listening to men talk about affairs as though adultery were not the problem, but the symptom of a problem. The affair may indicate a problem within the specific marital relationship or a more general problem that the man has in conducting relationships at all. In either case, an affair should be understood as a desperate although inappropriate solution to a problem that the adulterer can find no other way to solve on his own.

Many affairs can be attributed to a man's fear of intimacy or his inability to communicate his feelings and needs. In an affair, a man has more control than in a marriage: he can be as intimate with his lover as he wishes to be, and if the circumstances become uncomfortable he can go home. Lovers ask fewer questions than wives, so he is less likely to feel cornered emotionally. At home he can also get away with being less intimate, covering for himself, and thus divorcing himself from the pain of his dysfunctional marriage, even divorcing himself from himself.

Telling lies is easy for men: they have been trained to lie in order to conceal their deepest selves (the Lone Ranger), or to one-up others, or to defend their masculinity by inflating their successes and exploits (Vince Lombardi). In the case of affairs, a husband's not telling his wife what he is really thinking and feeling is a way of shutting her out of his inner reality. "Lying augments distance and space; only the liar knows the truth of the situation, and he is alone inside with his own special knowledge" (Scarf 1987, 165). An adulterous man has protected himself from his discomfort with his wife by taking as lover a woman who asks few questions and whom he can leave when he wishes. It is a desperate attempt to save his marriage by finding a new safe space, and a desperate attempt to save his privatized masculinity from invasive questions and pressures to be more real.

This is how a man views an affair if he is the adulterer. If his wife is the adulterer, his response is predictably different. Scarf points out that even when a man has deceived his wife in the past, he may be quick to apply a double standard when she is caught in an adulterous relationship: "I felt furious, betrayed; I felt as if I couldn't trust her! I felt that there was someone else out there who knew all about me, and who had, for that reason, triumphed! He had—even though I didn't know who he was—bested me, taken away something that was mine, exclusively!" (1987, 129).

A man's adulterous wife has set up a situation in which she has not only deceived her husband (men are used to being lied to by men, but not by women), but she has also, in a one-up-one-down world, created a situation in which her husband becomes obsessed over being bested by another man. This is fertile ground for a minister. The issues to be explored include a man's relation to his wife and his marital commitment, as well as his comprehension of his standing in relation to other men.

Less talked about in the pastoral care literature is a situation that ministers face more often now than in the past: a homosexual affair. Married men who lead some sort of homosexual life are more common than many ministers admit publicly (it is estimated that 30 percent of men who frequent gay bars are married), and the problems of such an affair are different from those of a heterosexual affair (Myers 1989, 147–68). Not only must the man in crisis deal with his wife's discovery of his affair, but with her discovery of his homosexuality as well, a subject that most American Christians still approach with a mixture of guilt and condemnation of self or others.

What the Minister Has to Offer

Maggie Scarf proposes an application of systems theory triangulation to explain why some affairs happen:

The Other Woman or the Other Man is, frequently, introduced into a situation as a means of handling otherwise unbearable tensions that exist within the marital relationship itself. The lover, although one doesn't tend to view his or her presence in this fashion, is often brought into the picture as a way of keeping a shaky twosome together when they're in danger of flying apart. Becoming involved with someone outside the relationship is, at times, similar to adding that third leg to a table that's about to fall over with a resounding crash. (1987, 146–47)

For this reason some affairs should be understood as desperate although inappropriate attempts to solve a problem between two married people. In such cases, the minister has the opportunity to encourage a healthier relationship between husband and wife.

In dealing with adulterous situations, whether hetero- or homosexual, the minister is wise to combine private conversations with conversations that include both spouses. In panic, men who hurt may believe that their only recourse is to run. Ministers have the opportunity in some cases to help save the relationship, insofar as adulterous situations are cries for help. When understood as desperate forms of triangulation, adulterous affairs suggest that more commitment is present in the marital relationship on the part of the adulterous husband than might at first be assumed.

MEN AND DIVORCE

Much of the literature on divorce paints divorcing or divorced men as villains, callous to the feelings of the wives and children they are abandoning. The experience of ministers suggests that such cold-heartedness is unusual in divorcing and divorced men. Men may be emotionally repressed or emotionally dysfunctional, but few are truly callous when it comes to their families. Of course there are fathers who flee their families, who shirk child-support payments and fail to exercise their visitation rights. But most divorced men seen by ministers in the church are responsible men, trying to come to terms with a family tragedy that has been as painful for them as for anyone else. For a minister to assume that divorcing fathers are irresponsible is a mistake.

Staying in Touch

"A divorce is like an amputation, you survive but there's less of you" (Atwood 1972, 42). Whatever does survive hurts for a long time. Mental health statistics belie the myth that divorcing men are unfeeling and uncaring. In a survey article of psychiatric literature on fathers and divorce, therapist John W. Jacobs concludes that whereas fathers who have frequent contact with their children following a divorce seem to heal more quickly than those who do not, men cannot always surmount the obstacles they put in their own way (1982, 1238). Men are nine times more likely to be admitted to a psychiatric hospital during the first year of separation or early divorce than men from intact homes; women are only three times more likely. The difficulty a minister faces is not in getting a man in crisis to admit his children's pain or their difficulty in adjusting, but in getting him to admit his own pain. To process a divorce, like so many other forms of reaching out for help, demands that a man learn to speak a vocabulary with which he is not immediately comfortable. He will probably have to redefine his masculinity, from a traditional set of assumptions to a more sensitive one, an identity that is able to use relationship wounds as an opportunity for new growth.

Over dinner one evening, I sat with my divorced friend Alan. After having custody of his teenage son, Alex, for a year, Alan had just completed a bitter custody battle with his ex-wife, during which the son decided to move back in with his mother. Alan looked distraught. Seeking to help, I asked him how he felt about Alex's having chosen to return to his mother. Alan answered with an analysis of why Alex had made a choice for the best. I asked again how Alan felt. This time he answered with a lengthy explanation of how tense things had been between him and Alex. A third time I asked, "Alan, how do *you feel* about the fact that Alex has moved back in with Elsa?" Alan looked at me as though he did not understand the question. Perhaps he did not. When asked to tell me his own feelings about what must have been a painful abandonment, he could not find any emotions to get in touch with.

Caring for Himself

Emotionally crippled men can barely take care of their own needs in crisis, and they are ill-equipped to be sensitive to the emotional needs of others. Not only is this a contributing factor to divorce as a marriage in trouble devolves into further emotional dysfunction, but it also hinders a man's postdivorce recovery. Ministers need to encourage men in crisis to find their own long-lost emotions. As well, ministers need to be willing to listen patiently as men go over and over the same material. When men are unused to expressing feelings but finally find them deep inside, they often must articulate them repeatedly in order to befriend these unfamiliar emotions.

Those going through a divorce often praise the exaggerated euphoria that initially follows divorce as being the freedom they had long sought. Deborah Tannen (1990, 40–41) points out, however, that when women describe the freedom that comes following a divorce, they use the synonyms independence and autonomy. When men describe this freedom, they praise the relief from claustrophobia and the new freedom from responsibility to answer to anyone. In other words, women describe a freedom into something, whereas men describe a freedom from something.

That men are less clear about what they are being freed into (rather than from) suggests the powerful lostness and loneliness many men feel once the initial euphoria has worn off. Ministers can predict that for up to two years, newly divorced men will try on a series of new "hats," new identities, as they sort out what it is they have been freed into, what new identity is appropriate for them to adopt as one single—again. Many of these temporary and alternative self-images will be variant forms of the inherited masculine gender-role stereotype: the male workaholic, the irresponsible roué, the once-a-week good-time dad, the feckless adventurer. Eventually this search for a comfortable self-identity settles down, but when it is slow to do so, men often rush back into marriage to find a new mate who will solve their problems for them and once again express their pent-up emotions.

WHEN A MARRIAGE BEGINS TO CHANGE

Change is endemic to the world, to Christianity, and to the human life cycle, "the ages of man." The natural shape of marriage is also one of change and flexibility. Yet change is often frightening for men, particularly when they fear the loss of their masculine identity in the process. As well, it is the nature of homeostatic systems to resist change, and hence change within a marital relationship may be angrily resisted. Changes assert one partner's essential differentness from the vision in the other partner's head. "This is why, in collusive marital systems, one spouse's effort to change will generally be blocked by the other or met with a rapid compensatory move directed toward restoring the system's customary equilibrium and balance" (Scarf 1987, 334). Ministers can greatly assist men in crisis by helping them come to terms with the fact that marriages change in shape and focus as naturally as does any other biological system.

Stages of Relationship Growth

Therapists Carol Nadelson, Derek Polansky, and Mary Alice Matthews suggest that marriage goes through five predictable stages. Each stage demands the acceptance of change and a readjustment on the part of both partners if the marital relationship is to retain healthy open communication and the possibility that both husband and wife will continue to find themselves empowered (Scarf 1987, 14–17).

The first stage of marriage they term *idealization,* in which all the mythical expectations are brought to the relationship and, through the blindness of enchantment, the faults of each partner are ignored or rationalized.

The second stage is termed *disappointment and disenchantment,* when husbands and wives come to the realization that they have married a human person, full of foibles and irritating habits, not always devoted to the self-sacrificial meeting of the other's needs. The sharp contrast between the expectations and the reality of marriage makes this stage a tough bump in a relationship, explaining in part why the average length of a marriage today is two years.

The third stage they call *productivity,* the stage in which much of the energy of both partners is turned outward toward children and career.

The fourth stage, *redefinition,* is characterized by the couple's devotion to launching their children out on their own, and by laying the groundwork for the second half of their lives as an economically stable couple with nonresident children.

The fifth stage is termed *reintegration and postparenting,* when husband and wife have become accepting of each other's personhood, recommit themselves to a growing and healthy relationship, and shift to senior status in preparation for grandchildren.

To Nadelson, Polansky, and Matthews's interpretation, one other time of change and potential crisis needs to be added, that of *retirement.* The tasks of adjusting to spending large blocks of time together and preparing for a good death need conscious intention.

Individuation within Marriage

When already emotionally dysfunctional men are locked into marital relationships that increase dysfunction through projective identification, what vision might a minister hold out for helping to make a marriage healthy and mutually respectful of the needs and dignity of both husband and wife?

Emotional interdependence within the bonds of a deeply committed relationship—the integration of independence and intimacy (Scarf 1987, 335–36)—is the goal for healthy marital life for both men and women. Integration assumes that men are as capable of doing emotional work as are women, and that women are as capable of providing and protecting as are men. Emotional independence within the bonds of a deeply committed relationship assumes an equality and a sharing that are unusual in marriage but not unattainable. In a healthy relationship, each partner has differentiated his or her own separate, distinct self from the family context in which that self developed.

Scarf (1987, 362–75) draws her readers' attention to the schema devised by therapist Stuart Johnson, by which couples can measure their progress on the road to a healthily individuated functioning within marriage. Johnson's schema outlines five possible ways in which intimate partners will be able to relate to each other—all highly dependent on the degree of separation and individuation that each member of the couple has achieved.

What Johnson calls a level 5 relationship, or *paradox,* is the least healthy relationship on his scale. In this interaction, the two major human needs—to be a separate self and to be emotionally connected to another human being—cannot possibly be met, for being close to a partner and not being close to a partner are equally terrifying prospects. Intimacy, in such an individual's world, is the negation of autonomy; autonomy is the negation of closeness. Both intimacy and independence feel dangerous, so that relationships tend to be difficult, transient, and unstable.

Johnson's level 4 relationship, or *projective identification,* describes the majority of marital relationships, in which a husband or wife takes ownership of one-half of the intimacy-independence polarity but not the other half. In this sort of relationship, one can be intimate or independent but not both, because intimacy and independence are still viewed as a mutually exclusive polarity. One partner in the marriage seeks warmth and openness, the other seeks distant boundaries and personal space. Because such couples have taken a single whole and divided it half and half, the overriding problem for both spouses is recognizing just where one person ends and the other begins. Their personalities are so merged that each must rely on the other not to change, for change would threaten the delicate balance that creates the wholeness of one personality but not two distinct individuals.

Level 3, according to Johnson, is called *conscious splitting.* From a minister's point of view, married couples at this stage have begun to opt for a healthier relationship, but only part of the time. When they fight they descend to level

4; when they calm down and apologize, they ascend to level 2 by admitting their own ambiguities about the place of each in the intimacy-independence polarity. What is introduced at level 3 is an increasing awareness of complexity—a dilemma within the self as well as a dilemma involving the intimate partner.

Level 2 couples, or those *tolerating ambivalence,* are able to express their need for both intimacy and independence to each other as conflicting forces that exist inside each person's own head, but neither is quite comfortable with his or her own needs or those of the other. Respecting the other spouse's needs for both intimacy and independence is something they are able to do for each other sacrificially, but always at the price of conscious decision, rather than as a manner of being.

The healthiest couples, at level 1, are said to be *integrated.* They perceive autonomy and intimacy as states of being—not spatial positions on a closeness-distance ruler, as in level 2. At level 1, intimacy and autonomy are perceived as the way the members of the couple are rather than what activities each chooses to offer the other. At this level of integration, a couple's intimate relationship takes the form of a dialogue between separate yet deeply committed beings rather than fusion and interpersonal merger, as it does in the less differentiated levels.

Components of a Healthy Marriage

What allows marriages to survive change and grow into deeper levels of intimacy? In a schema unrelated but complementary to Johnson's, therapists William Lederer and Don Jackson (1968, passim) enumerate four component ingredients for a healthy marriage: (1) an unquestioned and unshakable commitment by the couple to remain together, facing the challenges of marriage in the faith that their pledge is forever; (2) an attitude of flexibility that understands that change is a part of the normal marital cycle as well as individual human growth, and that over the course of time, individuals can be helped to make those choices that are correct for them; (3) a genuine interest in one another, seeking the other's welfare above all else, and willing to find activities that give real pleasure to both members of the couple; and (4) an unbounded sense of humor, laughing first of all at the comedy of one's own human condition, and laughing with the other's self-laughter. These four components form practical suggestions for working out how to be two separate yet deeply committed individuals in dialogue, balancing independence and intimacy to the advantage of both.

These are goals for the minister of men in crisis. The first job is to get men to own their feelings and express them. From there the minister can build and educate and listen to men as they choose to claim healthy interdependence.

6

LOVE AND FRIENDSHIP NEEDS

In *Women in Love*, D. H. Lawrence explores the complicated relationships between two close sisters, Ursula and Gudrun, and two close friends, Rupert and Gerald. Rupert and Ursula fall in love and marry, whereas Gerald and Gudrun carry on a passionate love affair. When Ursula perceives how deeply Rupert has been affected and changed by his friendship with Gerald, she confronts him:

> "You've got me," she said. "Why should you *need* others? Why must you force people to agree with you? Why can't you be single by yourself, as you are always saying? You try to bully Gerald—as you tried to bully Hermione. You must learn to be alone. And it's so horrid of you. You've got me. And yet you want to force other people to love you as well. You do try to bully them to love you. And even then you don't want their love."
>
> His face was full of real perplexity.
>
> "Don't I?" he said. "It's the problem I can't solve. I *know* I want a perfect and complete relationship with you: and we've nearly got it—we really have. But beyond that. *Do* I want a real, ultimate relationship with Gerald? Do I want a final, almost extra-human relationship with him—a relationship in the ultimate of me and him—or don't I?"
>
> She looked at him for a long time with strange bright eyes, but she did not answer. (1975, 355)

WHAT FRIENDSHIP IS NOT

In a marital relationship, a husband and wife need to achieve a healthy emotional interdependence, not a symbiotic merging of identities that debilitates each. Some of each partner's emotional needs will have to be met outside their marriage, and these generally take the form of same-gender friendships. Such friendships are more common among women than men because men do not yet comprehend the value of same-gender friendships. The value escapes men's attention because of what they fear about such close relations.

Friendship Is Not Homosexual

Society's punitive patriarchs raise suspicions of homosexuality whenever two men, such as Rupert and Gerald, become close friends. This has come home to me in an odd sort of way: My book, *New Adam,* offers a lengthy treatment of the relationship between Jonathan and David (1 Samuel 18—2 Samuel 1). Jonathan's father, King Saul, misinterprets the friendship as being unhealthy and so does his best to destroy it, but instead he destroys his son in the process (1992, 75–90). Even though I took care to point out that I was not speaking about a homosexual relationship, nevertheless a handful of reviewers accused me publicly of writing gay theology.

The eyes of patriarchal prejudice are everywhere: I am now aware that any discussion of men's friendship must deal with the issue of homosexuality and then set it aside as a paradigm quite different from the nongenital emotional commitment between two male adults. This chapter neither advocates nor justifies homosexual relationships between men; it simply shows how ministers can help men in crisis become healthier and have happier marriages by encouraging men to develop supportive emotional commitments to other male friends.

To set aside the subject of homosexuality is not to agree with patriarchy, and a few comments on its nature need to be made. The literature is growing rapidly and mostly centers on whether homosexuality is the product of nature or nurture or some combination. Denominations have largely entered the discussion at this same point, often seeking to determine whether homosexual persons can become ordained and serve as spiritual leaders, and (more recently) whether the military should permit acknowledged homosexuals to continue service. More than a little wisdom resides with those who wish the churches would expend their energy instead on mission, evangelism, and the pastoral care of their (many times dwindling) memberships. (For two respected treatments of homosexuality and the Christian tradition, see William Countryman, *Dirt, Greed, and Sex: Sexual Ethics in the New Testament and Their Implications for Today* [Philadelphia: Fortress Press, 1988]; and Robin Scroggs, *The New Testament and Homosexuality* [Philadelphia: Fortress Press, 1983].)

Homosexuality Is Not to Be Feared

Many ministers will never hear directly of men's homosexual genital experiences because most men, even many gay men, bury these experiences deep within their most privates lives. They have learned by way of the church's recent hysteria on the subject that it is dangerous to speak of homosexuality in the Christian community, even to ministers. Ministers will, however, see both the side-effects of hidden homosexual activity and men's fears of being incorrectly accused of such activity.

The fear of homosexuality is termed *homophobia* — the fear of coming in contact with a homosexual or, more commonly, the fear of what might happen if a person becomes emotionally committed to another of the same gender (Rist 1992). As our society changes, more men will come to realize that homosexual men have not chosen homosexuality but are attempting to understand it as a given. Nevertheless, many men still fear that they might be unable to establish committed same-gender friendships, heterosexual to heterosexual. This fear takes one of three forms.

Being out of control of his body. A man's anxiety over being out of control of his own body is not the same fear as being raped or sexually violated—fears with which women have needed to cope since creation. Most adult men are physically able to repel unwanted sexual advances. Rather, this fear is an extension of a cultural myth that when a man gets aroused in some way he is no longer able to control his physical urges—he becomes irrational. Thus, the expression of homophobia among men is their own fear of their own bodies. If they should somewhere find another man to be warm and caring, they might lose control of themselves sexually and embarrass themselves or lose face through some act or gesture they have been taught is a contradiction of their masculinity.

Fearing vulnerability to other men. Men fear intimate friendships with other men because they fear the powerful ways other men might abuse them emotionally if they make themselves vulnerable. Men's lifelong experience of other men, at school or at the place of business, is that they must always make themselves one-up; the only other choice is to be one-down. Even though men may not fear specific friends per se, their life experience with men in general is negative enough to override their willingness to take risks in many cases.

Perceiving intimacy as claustrophobic. If a man has a limited emotional repertoire, he will have a limited ability to deal with his own needs and feelings. In turn, this will give him little energy to deal with requests from spouses or friends for support and assistance. Not to make close friends is then a form of self-protection, a husbanding of limited resources, all of which proceeds from a man's lifelong repression of his feelings, emotions, and needs for intimacy as a product of patriarchy's training in what it means to be appropriately masculine.

WHAT FRIENDSHIP IS

Friendship offers the richness of engaging another without romantic complication or expectation, and thus committed friendship can be the purest form of friendship available to men and women. Friendship is the arena in which an "I" is called into being, for no "I" can exist until it has been confronted by an Other in relationship to which the self discovers its own being and borders. For this reason, classical Greek culture and many early Christian writers counted friendship between adult males to be the highest source of human virtue (Culbertson and Shippee 1990, 148–49; Culbertson 1992, chap. 6).

Friendship as a Human Virtue

In Book Eight of his *Nicomachean Ethics,* Aristotle discusses the male motivation to friendship: to be friends, men must (1) feel goodwill toward each other, (2) be aware of each other's goodwill, and (3) each possess qualities that are lovable to the other. He then goes on to identify three types or classes of male-male friendship, each of which presumes the above three qualifications, but each of which exists in order to satisfy a different purpose. The first type Aristotle calls *friendship of utility,* which may take the form of helping each other with professional problems, car-pooling, authoring a project together, or giving advice (although this is not to be confused with a mentoring situation or a teacher-student relationship). As Aristotle points out, such relationships do not necessarily carry any sense of love for the other, for ultimately the investment in the relationship is self-serving and seeks personal benefit under the guise of friendship. When there is nothing to be gained, no favor to be done, no mutual goal to be achieved, such friends spend less time together, and thus the two friends drift apart when the benefits begin to decrease.

The second type of friendship Aristotle discusses is *friendship of pleasure*. This too has a strong self-serving element, for as he points out, "we enjoy the society of witty people not because of what they are in themselves, but because they are agreeable to us." These friendships have more emotion in them than the utilitarian type, although they are prone to a certain fragility or transience as our emotional needs or our tastes and preferences change. Even this type is somewhat unusual for adult men; it is more typical of young men who simply "hang out" together and enjoy each other's company. For many adult men, however, the idea of simply being together to experience the pure pleasure of each other's company, without women or any socially acceptable justification, is frightening.

The third type of friendship Aristotle discusses is *perfect friendship*. This is the highest and least common form of friendship. Aristotle understands that such a relationship involves a commitment to a mutually held set of values and a willingness to be emotionally intimate. Each wishes the good of the other above his own personal good. Each is in service to the other without desire for reciprocity. Each enjoys the pleasure of the other innocently and absolutely. Each is healthy enough to recognize the good in the other because he recognizes the good in himself. Such a relationship is the perfect form of community between two men and is characterized by sayings such as "Friends have one soul between them," and "A friend is another self."

MEN AND FRIENDSHIP

At the end of chapter 2 of Lawrence's *Women in Love*, Rupert and Gerald comprehend subconsciously that they wish to risk an intimate friendship with each other, but the intensity of feelings between these two heterosexual friends frightens them. As Lawrence describes it:

> There was a pause of strange enmity between the two men, that was very near to love. It was always the same between them; always their talk brought them into a deadly nearness of contact, a strange, perilous intimacy which was either hate or love, or both. They parted with apparent unconcern, as if their going apart were a trivial occurrence. And they really kept it to the level of trivial occurrence. Yet the heart of each burned from the other. They burned with each other, inwardly. This they would never admit. They intended to keep their relationship a casual free-and-easy friendship, they were not going to be so unmanly and unnatural as to allow any heart-burning between them. They had not the faintest belief in deep relationship between men and men, and their disbelief prevented any development of their powerful but suppressed friendliness. (1975, 28)

Conditioned to believe that deep intimate friendship between two men is "unmanly and unnatural," the two men attempt to juggle their friendship in such a way that it remains minimally committed and intimate, each hoping that the other will not notice how much need for friendship is already there, crying out to be met.

Risking Friendship

When asked who their best friends are, most women name other women they talk to regularly. Studies of men and friendship reach the same conclusion over and over again: the majority of adult males do not have friends. Backed into a corner, some married men describe their wives as friends but will also articulate feelings of loneliness, knowing well that when one's circle of support is limited to only one friend, life can seem quite isolated (Tannen 1990, 80). Women have all-purpose friends; men have sequential friends, that is, friends who are compartmentalized so that one is a fishing buddy, one a car-pool buddy, one a lunch-at-the-office buddy, and one a poker buddy. The compartmentalization keeps anyone from ever knowing too much about a man.

Some of the problems that interfere with men's friendships have been enumerated above. An additional problem is that men are not conditioned by their life experience to do the forms of risk-taking or the intimate exchanges that make friendships possible. Conversations designed to deliver information or impart opinions do not make for deep commitments. Tannen tells the story of her single male friend who had lost his wide circle of friends after he became involved with a woman:

> I had a friend, a man, who had been single for many years and had developed a wide and strong network of women friends to whom he talked frequently. When he developed a stable relationship with a woman and they moved in together, his friends complained that he did not tell them anything anymore. "It's not that I'm keeping things from them," he told me. "It's just that Naomi and I get along fine and there's nothing to tell." By saying this, he did, however, tell me about a problem in his relationships — although it involved not his partner but his friends. (1990, 99)

Silently and alone, men go about their business. If they do not talk, they cannot keep friendships alive. If they do talk, they reveal themselves, becoming vulnerable and fearful. So they place other priorities first, priorities from which they have been carefully trained to shore up their masculine identity. As one writer puts it: "Maintaining one's lawn is more important than maintaining one's friendships" (Letich 1991, 86). Or they try to force friendship into unnatural patterns designed to conform to the one-up-one-down competitiveness by which men are trained to deal with other men (Pittman 1990, 46).

Six Types of Friendship

We all develop many different types of friends and acquaintances over the course of our lives. We develop friendships of various levels of intensity with men and with women, with young and old. In *Necessary Losses,* Judith Viorst divides friendships into six categories:

Convenience friends. These are the neighbors, office mates, or car-poolers whose lives routinely intersect with ours—the people with whom we exchange small favors. They drive our children to soccer when we are sick. They keep our dog for a week when we go on vacation. When we need a lift they offer a ride to the garage to pick up our car. With convenience friends, we never come too close or tell too much: we maintain our public face and emotional distance. "Which means," says Russell, "that I'll talk about being overweight but not about being depressed, or being mad but not being blind with rage, pinched for money this month but never that I'm worried sick."

Some men place severe limits on the number of convenience friends they have, for it is hard for some men to ask for help. To request help places the other in the one-up position, automatically placing the asker in the one-down position. It makes the asker beholden and therefore vulnerable. This threat to masculine independence means a man is not self-sufficient, not able to solve the problem that has presented itself. A man will risk cutting his finger off in a power saw before asking another man to help him hold the board.

Special-interest friends. These friendships depend on the sharing of some activity or concern. There are sports friends, work friends, gym friends, clean-green friends. "I'd say that what we're doing together is doing together, not being together," Stephen says of his weekly tennis partner. As with convenience friends, we can be regularly involved with special-interest friends without being intimate.

Historical friends. With luck we also have a friend who knew us back when. The years have passed, we have gone separate ways, we have little in common now, but we still are an intimate part of each other's past.

One of my friends describes certain of her friendships, including ours, as "a narrative friendship"—a friendship in which we get together occasionally to tell each other stories about who we are and what has happened or is happening to us. Narrative friendships gain their power over a number of years as the stories accumulate. Men like telling stories; they have learned that it draws attention to themselves, provides a forum for them to recount their own achievements, disarms others who might be more powerful by causing them to laugh, and gives men control over how much they reveal about themselves by the way they shape the story. Ministers in the Christian community will be aware of how important storytelling is in the forming of Christian identity, and so have a feel for how important storytelling is for many men's identities.

Crossroad friends. Like historical friends, our crossroad friends are important for what was—for a friendship shared at a crucial, now past, time of life: a time, perhaps, when they roomed in college together, or served a stint in the U.S. Air Force together, or worked as eager young singles in Manhattan together. With historical friends and crossroad friends links are forged that are

strong enough to endure with not much more contact than once-a-year letters at Christmas, maintaining a special intimacy—dormant but always ready
to be revived—on those rare but tender occasions when the two friends meet.
For most men, historical and crossroad friends are little more than fond
memories, although if you ask a man to name his best male friend, he will
almost always name someone from his past, usually someone he has not seen
or spoken to in several years. Men are slow to understand how laughable is
the idea that one can have a best friend with whom no information has been
shared for a long time. However, as we shall see, these sorts of fondly remembered friends can be of great use to ministers in helping men change their
friendship patterns.

Cross-generational friends. Another intimacy—tender but unequal—exists in
the friendships that form across generations, the younger enlivening the
older, the older instructing the younger. Each role, as mentor or quester, as
adult or child, offers gratifications of its own. Men in the men's movement
are discovering the important role of a mentor in a man's life, a powerful example of cross-generational friends. A mentor fills the important role of
father and guide to men who have poor relations with their own fathers or
whose fathers have died. Being a mentor provides a special sense of fulfillment for a man whose children have left home, turned away from him, or
have disparaged him. Throughout history, the role of mentor has been a
common one, although more recently it has been ignored. Yet we find it still
effective; for example, in the professor-student interaction, the coach-athlete
relationship, the Big Brother program, the priest-teen mentoring, the spiritual director-directee interdependence.

Close friends. Emotionally and physically, we maintain a few ongoing friendships of deep intimacy. Although we may not expose as much (or the same
kinds of things) to each of our closest friends, close friendships involve revealing aspects of our private self—our feelings and thoughts, our wishes and
fears and fantasies and dreams—We reveal ourselves not only by telling but
also by wordlessly showing what we are, the unattractive as well as the nice.
"To be her friend," said a friend of the late political activist and writer Jenny
Moore, "was to be for a little while as good as you wish you were."

MAKING FRIENDS

At a ski resort in Switzerland where the two couples have gone on holiday,
Gerald's relationship with Gudrun crumbles as soon as Rupert and Ursula
leave them to return home. In a rage of jealousy at Gudrun's flirtation with a
young Italian, Gerald confronts the two and then wanders off into the gla-
ciers where he freezes to death. Both Gudrun and Rupert are deeply affected
by Gerald's death, although Ursula has already tired of Gerald's manipulation
of others. She also cannot understand Rupert's fascination with Gerald, his
need for male friendship outside of their marriage.

Gudrun went to Dresden. She wrote no particulars of herself. Ursula stayed at
the Mill with Birkin for a week or two. They were both very quiet.
   "Did you need Gerald?" she asked one evening.
   "Yes," he said.
   "Aren't I enough for you?" she asked.
   "No," he said. "You are enough for me, as far as a woman is concerned. You are
all women to me. But I wanted a man friend, as eternal as you and I are eternal."
   "Why aren't I enough?" she said. "You are enough for me. I don't want any-
body else but you. Why isn't it the same with you?"
   "Having you, I can live all my life without anybody else, any other sheer
intimacy. But to make it complete, really happy, I wanted eternal union with a
man too: another kind of love," he said.
   "I don't believe it," she said. "It's an obstinacy, a theory, a perversity."
   "Well—" he said.
   "You can't have two kinds of love. Why should you!"
   "It seems as if I can't," he said. "Yet I wanted it."
   "You can't have it, because it's false, impossible," she said.
   "I don't believe that," he answered. (Lawrence 1975, 472–73)

Even after realizing how destructive his relationship with Gerald was, Rupert
is unable to give up his conviction that male friendship meets a need in men
that cannot be met in marriage.

Six Steps to Friendship

In counseling men, a minister may discover the need for specific help in developing friendships, because men have such limited experience in this area.
The building up of friendships is a long, slow process. The impatient careseeker should not undertake it and the impatient minister should not suggest
it. But for those men who are willing to take risks in exploring the fulfillment
that comes from same-gender friendships, the following six steps, adapted
from suggestions by Larry Letich (1991, 87), may be helpful:

1. The careseeker must want friendships badly enough to pursue them. To
   find a good, long-term committed friendship can be as difficult as finding
   a job or a sexual relationship. This may cause the careseeker some anxiety,
   for pursuing friendship with another man contradicts the myth of male
   self-sufficiency. Letich remarks, "You have to remind yourself often that
   there's nothing weird or effeminate about wanting a friend." If married,
   the careseeker should share with his wife and children the fact that he is
   setting out to broaden his network of support by making a male friend.
   Perhaps his wife or children might suggest someone who would be an appropriate candidate. If the careseeker has sons, this can set an example for
   them about the importance of friendships that will help counteract the patriarchal rigidity most boys still grow up with.
2. Identify a possible friend. Men in men's groups and others who seem in
   some way to be questioning society's view of masculinity and success are
   possible candidates. Do not look for men so overcommitted or influential

that they never have a moment to themselves. Possible sources of friendship could be the careseeker's religious community, civic organizations, or recreational sports clubs. It often helps if the careseeker picks someone with whom he has more than one thing in common—for instance, both could be married and have a mutual hobby or sport or commitment to the church—but this does not always have to be the case. Men already have a tendency to spend time with people like themselves, but there is a great deal to be learned from close friends with whom one does not have identical interests and values.

Like historical friends, crossroad friends are a fertile ground for ministers who are seeking to help men develop the grace of more intimate friendships. Because so many men, when asked who their male friends are, identify someone from their past, the minister might suggest that the careseeker reconnect with an old friend, someone remembered particularly fondly. Recounting memories and retelling stories may be good places for men who feel awkward being friends to start opening up to each other.

3. Think through ways in which getting to know each other will be easy and attractive. An opening line of "Hey, I want to be your friend, let's do lunch" may easily scare off a prospective friendship. Instead, the friends should at first get involved in some sort of non-work-related mutual interest or project. This could be something as simple as going fishing together, or a more complicated project such as building a new cabinet for the altar guild. Two men need structured time just to be together, to size each other up, to get used to each other without the pressure of being "friends."

4. Invite the new friend to stop for a cup of coffee or a beer. Ask personal questions. Find out about his girlfriend or his wife and his children or his job. Find out what frustrates him or rewards him in his life. Look for common likes and dislikes. The seeker must also risk being personal about himself as well. These conversations should build slowly over a period of time, each time risking a little more honesty.

5. After a few months of shared activity and cups of coffee, the friends should arrange to meet at least once a month, even if for only a few hours. The seeker should expect to be the caller and arranger, especially in the beginning. The minister should remember that some men are in the habit of keeping track of "points scored" in their relationship with other men; this habit must be overcome. If another man does not wish to be friends, he will make that obvious and the seeker should look elsewhere.

6. Eventually the two men should sit down and talk openly about their friendship. It may take time to reach this point, but while it is typical for men to leave things unsaid, this step is crucial. In a society that treats friendships as replaceable, one has to go against the tide by declaring the value of this special friendship to the other, and sharing the value of that friendship with one's own family. Only then will the friendship survive patriarchy's prejudices and life's stresses, such as a serious disagreement or one of the friends moving away.

What the Minister Has to Offer

Gerald's frozen body is brought back from the glacier and laid out in the ski chalet where the two couples had been vacationing. Gudrun is unable to keep the wake due to her shock and confusion. Rupert, however, makes regular visits to the body, in an attempt to sort out his feelings about the death of the man he believed to be his best friend.

> "I didn't want it to be like this—I don't want it to be like this," he cried to himself. . . .
> Suddenly he was silent. But he sat with his head dropped to hide his face. Then furtively he wiped his face with his fingers. Then suddenly he lifted his head and looked straight at Ursula with dark, almost vengeful eyes.
> "He should have loved me," he said. "I offered him."
> She, afraid, white, with mute lips, answered:
> "What difference would it have made!"
> "It would!" he said. "It would."
> He forgot her and turned to look at Gerald. With head oddly lifted, like a man who draws his head back from an insult, half haughtily, he watched the cold, mute material face. It had a bluish cast. It sent a shaft like ice through the heart of the living man. Cold, mute, material! Birkin remembered how once Gerald had clutched his hand with a warm, momentaneous grip of final love. For one second—then let go again, let go for ever. If he had kept true to that clasp, death would not have mattered. Those who die, and dying still can love, still believe, do not die. They live still in the beloved. Gerald might still have been living in the spirit with Birkin, even after death. He might have lived with his friend, a further life. (Lawrence 1975, 471)

Rupert believes that had Gerald been able to make a commitment of friendship that continued to grow, perhaps Gerald's death could have been prevented. But the commitment between the two men was neither equal nor complementary. Rupert wanted something out of the relationship that Gerald could not, or would not, give him.

In counseling men, the minister may also discover that the male careseeker wishes something out of the relationship that the minister is unable or unwilling to provide. The minister needs to be clear in his or her own mind about what relationship is appropriate and which relationships are not. If the minister is a man, the careseeker may confuse him with his father and work out inappropriate needs for love and attention, or even become angry and rebellious (Hopcke 1990, 170). The careseeker, finding unconditional positive regard from another man for the first time, may assume that the minister is going to become his best friend. If the minister is a woman, the careseeker may approach her with sexual signals or sexual needs, because this is the way many men are conditioned to react to women in situations of emotional intimacy. The point of counseling is not that the seeker learn to love the minister, but that the seeker learn to love himself. As Hopcke points out, "To love yourself after all means learning how to love a man, not a woman" (1990, 104).

7

MASCULINE SPIRITUALITY

In the "About Men" column of the *New York Times Magazine*, novelist Dan Wakefield wrote of the panic he has felt when asked about his prayer life, or worse, when asked to pray in public. Real men, he had felt until recently, were supposed to "stand on their own two feet" and refrain from bowing their head, except once a week at sanctioned services. Relaxing his standards of masculine expectations and risking the laughter of his friends, Wakefield joined a prayer group:

> The women in a prayer group I belong to (it meets for an hour after work every Monday evening) told me they thought men had a harder time with prayer than they did, attributing the difficulty to a quality that prayer requires that they felt most men don't possess or cultivate much: humility. This explanation that seemed obvious to them had never occurred to me; my own humility consciousness was raised on the spot. (1988, 14)

Men have trouble with humility because of their performance-orientation. Performances of necessity generate pride, or at least self-assurance. Humility does not, by definition. Therapist Robert Hopcke observes:

> In turning to organized religion, many men find simply an ontological recapitulation of the one-sidedness and lack of creativity that landed them in their psychological predicament in the first place. The institutional church, therefore, may be simply one more instrument of alienation, rather than a place of deep self-knowing. (1990, 6)

To many in our society, the church seems to be out of touch with the human soul. It offers answers to questions that are not being asked but ignores the questions that are. It seems to care more about conformity and doctrine than about the struggles of men and women to find new ways to live together in an equality and justice expressive of God's love. It seems to have turned its back on the sufferings of the oppressed, siding instead with the patriarchal establishment. The church seems so protective of the past that it has sacrificed its own future.

MUSCULAR CHRISTIANITY

Around the turn of this century, a sequence of books appeared on the subject of masculine Christianity. In these books, often designed to train a young man in the way he should grow (Prov. 22:6), Christ himself was portrayed as "the supremely manly man," athletic and aggressive when necessary, but never a "Prince of Peace-at-any-price." One early model is found in *Tom Brown's Schooldays* by Thomas Hughes; another was the life of C. T. Studd, a successful cricketeer who left as a missionary to China on a combined platform of sports prowess and evangelism. In this literature, masculinity as a social construct was wed to Christology, and one's manhood, even in the church, was measured by the standards of stubborn courage, sacrifice without consideration for cost or pain, virile authority, and conformity to the behavior expected of those who would lead the world to a new Jerusalem.

The church, in its original vision defined as an inclusive community, was by the turn of this century so overlaid with patriarchy that the Christ who challenged the assumptions of his own society had been nearly obliterated, along with his promises that everything would be made new, replaced instead by a Christ who so affirmed the gender-values of his society that he became a caricature of himself. From a vision of an inclusive community of justice and equality in which every man and woman reflect fully the image of God, and in which oppression is so absent that there is neither male nor female (Gal. 3:28), the church has steadily degenerated to its present position of societal irrelevance.

To many persons today, the institutional church appears narrow and abusive, designed to defend the continuing rule of patriarchy over women, children, the elderly, and the already-oppressed. Interestingly, New Testament research suggests that these same groups—women, children, the elderly, and the oppressed—formed the primary composition of the early diaspora church. Twenty centuries later, the similarity of composition is striking. The difference between the church then and the church now, however, is that local Christian communities then were not ruled over by an exclusive authoritarian patriarchy, but by a largely lay ministry raised up within local communities and often disproportionately influenced by pious elderly women (Thurston 1989). Aristocratic Roman males both mocked and feared Christianity as a woman's religion. Two thousand years later, the Western church's membership is still primarily female, even though its visible ordained ministry no longer is.

Oppression in the Name of Christ

When patriarchs fear women and antipatriarchs and the oppressed who call them to responsibility, they attempt to exercise even firmer control. "Patriarchy arises out of an impoverished sense of the masculine as well as the feminine. A patriarchal system of control is set up when men fear the power, not only of women, but of other men" (Healy 1992, 141). Whereas the church no longer has the authority to burn people at the stake or to anathematize them literally, it can still do so figuratively by refusing people the right to exercise creative ministries, by withholding communion from them, by slandering them, by exiling them from what the church defines as the community of the faithful. Above all, the church anathematizes those who ask questions that are too hard. The institutional church succumbs repeatedly to the temptation to deny pastoral care to those whom the patriarchs fear.

The second Lubavitcher Rebbe made the following confession regarding his own emotional life:

> The basis by which I can listen to people's problems, sins and worries is that I can always look into myself and find a disposition for the same problem within me. The last disciple I listened to told me such a heinous story that I could not find any similarity to his life within me. And upon that realization, I was mortified, because this not only meant that such a similarity did exist, but that it lay deeply repressed within me. (Katz 1985, 75)

Patriarchal leadership in the church does not wish to look deep within itself at all that is repressed, all the dysfunction that is hidden and explained away. It is easier to banish from the community those who make the leadership uncomfortable, to silence the voices within who ask questions that are too hard, to remind women that their voices are unwelcomed, to reassert the value of muscular Christianity.

But according to the wisdom of the Lubavitcher Rebbe, at the moment that we do not recognize God in our neighbor, whoever that neighbor may be, we are forced to draw the conclusion that we know neither ourselves nor, more shatteringly, God. If I cannot see God in you, then there is not something wrong with you but something wrong with me and with my relationship to God. God encompasses much more than our human tendency to limitation would easily allow.

Doing as Better than Being

One way in which the patriarchal church has been able to maintain control is by promoting standards of piety that are visibly measurable. If we measure a Christian's worth by acts of good works, the number of parish and diocesan committees served, the level of church financial support, the willingness to volunteer, or the visible success of his or her prayer, then we have applied patriarchal standards of productivity to a soul-world wherein such measures are anathema. This is why Mother Teresa has repeatedly shunned recognition; she knows that a Christian is measured on the basis of being, rather than doing.

The doing-being polarity is perhaps the hardest confusion to tackle when engaged in spiritual counseling with men in crisis. A former parishioner wrote me something like the following:

> Ellen and I had a mega-fight in the last week or so and are still trying to repair the damage. I think it will take a long time. Our tolerance level for one another had just hit zero, so a little thing set off a big, big explosion. I told Jules, my shrink, about it and about how Ellen and I don't seem to communicate in the same language. (Ellen: "What can I do? I've done everything I know how to do." Me: "It's not a question of doing. It's a question of being. If you quit trying to do so damn much, maybe you could just be what you want to be." Ellen: "What

the hell are you talking about?") Jules got out his prescription pad (the first time he's ever done that) and wrote a prescription that said "A good life is the best revenge." We then talked about how I could try to be myself in marriage. It was interesting to contrast that with the advice Ellen got from her shrink. He suggested all sorts of things she could try. Things to do. To do. Lordy, lordy.

As in the church, so this married couple was struggling with conflicting values of being versus doing. Atypically, in this case it was the husband who valued being, and the wife who valued doing.

Teaching Men to "Be"

Because none of us is static, however, *being* does involve certain types of doing. Pastoral counselor David Augsburger describes the purpose of counseling, whether professional or pastoral, as threefold: (1) choice, such as whether to marry, divorce, change jobs, get more education; (2) change, such as the need to acquire new social skills, learn new ways of relating and resolving conflict, alter one's daily routine of activities, give up limiting dependencies, habits, addictions, or face a terminal illness; (3) clarity, the need to reduce confusion by gaining a realistic view of one's abilities and vocational possibilities, to reorient one's life while coming off drugs, or gain new perspectives on boundaries, responsibilities, and conflictual or entangled relationships.

Augsburger continues, "these metaphors are parallel to theological presuppositions that being is more essential to enabling growth than doing, that presence is more evocative of change than strategy, that calling persons to change (repentance), choice (responsibility), and clarity (integrity) are central to the counseling task" (1986, 350). Most men have *done* for so long that they have forgotten how to *be*. In the course of forgetting, they have also forgotten the God of long-suffering presence, who has promised simply to be with us, even to the end of time (Matt. 28:20).

HOPE FOR THE MINISTERS

Growing quietly within the larger Christian community, there are signs of hope and resurrection in the available new alternatives for ministers who work with men.

Biblical Exegesis

The first resource upon which a minister can draw in listening to men is the many new kinds of alternative exegesis now being done within the community of the faithful. For the first time, voices long silent or ignored in the text are being heard, through the work of feminist scholars such as Phyllis Trible, Elisabeth Schüssler Fiorenza, Mieke Bal, and Rebecca Chopp. Different messages are being given voice by the liberation theologians such as Paulo Freire, Leonardo Boff, Gustavo Guttierez, and Juan Luis Segundo. Theologians such as Carter Heyward, Sallie McFague, and Herb Richardson are developing whole theologies of friendship, providing new possibilities for finding God at work within deep emotional commitments to others.

Men's voices other than the patriarchal are being heard in the church, such as James Nelson, John Carmody, Merle Longwood, and Richard Rohr. As I have tried to show in my own *New Adam,* the recounting and discussion of alternative voices in the biblical text can be of great support as ministers seek to help men throw off the shackles of oppression and the confining strictures of patriarchy-generated gender-role stereotypes. Jonathan and David formed a deeply committed heterosexual friendship; Job sought the counsel of other men when his life went sour; Jesus nurtured his male followers through physical touch. These examples show the value of attending carefully to the biblical text in order that a minister might listen more effectively to changing men.

Creation Spirituality

Second, the development of creation theology and the Christian community's focus on environmental issues as an expression of our proper stewardship of creation lay the groundwork for ministers to discuss with men the stewardship of their own bodies, minds, and relationships. Long schooled to assume their dominion over creation, men need encouragement to cherish the beauty around them—to protect, not destroy it.

In helping men to steward their minds and bodies, ministers can encourage them to balance better their physical exercise and their quietude. Most men need more of both. Pastoral theologian James Griffiss articulates a theology of caring that is applicable to men's care for both their bodies and their spirits:

> Another image for caring that can be helpful is that of being aware of something or someone. While riding in a crowded train or bus I have often thought about the relationship between caring and awareness. In a crowd I can be aware of other people in several ways; as a possible threat to my life, which is a reaction of fear; as an inconvenience when they push against me, which is annoyance; and merely as other bodies, which is indifference. But there can also be those rare occasions when I am aware of someone as a person for whom I care or could care or ought to care—an elderly person or one who is ill, or one who seems attractive and interesting. Usually, in a crowd, awareness of another person offers no opportunity for caring, but in other situations, to become aware of someone creates the possibility for caring. Awareness can lead to caring; unawareness is the opposite of caring. So also is forgetting. To be unaware of a person or to forget him or her is the opposite of caring because it means I am refusing to welcome another; I am choosing not to reach out or to remember or hope for another. (1985, 88)

To ignore our own bodies and spirits is to refuse to welcome them as gifts from God. Instead, many men approach their bodies with an attitude of indifference or inconvenience or even fear. Men's refusal to listen to others, and to women in particular, can reveal an attitude of indifference or inconvenience or even fear, especially with regard to minds that are more alive and curious.

Theologies of Liberation

Third, liberation theology lays the groundwork for ministers to talk to men about their emerging identities once they have been freed from oppression by the patriarchs. Any concern for the liberation of men and women from customary stereotypes, as well as the changing mores in our society in regard to sexual activity, can be threatening to traditionalists. To them, such liberation represents the overthrow of a structured and comfortable hierarchy and the denial of what has long been regarded as natural and lawful in society. As any pastor knows, however, simply because such matters are threatening and disturbing does not mean they will go away or that we shall be able to return to what many would prefer to imagine as a golden age.

Women who say it is not part of the natural order of things that they should be or act in certain prescribed ways need to be cared for and, in turn, to care for others in a manner that enables them to realize their dreams of justice and equality. Those men who are more and more resistant to being classified and judged by received standards of masculinity need a different kind of caring than did their fathers. What it means to be a woman or a man now appears to be something to be discovered or achieved on one's own terms, so that in a caring relationship there may be less concern for preserving intact an unchallenged continuity with past values and patterns of behavior, and more concern for future possibilities (see James Griffiss's remarks on the liberation model of pastoral care cited in the Preface). Certainly a concern for the future has always been a dimension of serious pastoral care, but it has now become more explicit, more demanding.

TO MINISTERS WHO OFFER SPIRITUAL DIRECTION

In addition to the many counseling suggestions given in the previous pages, the creative minister will find certain techniques helpful when acting as a spiritual friend to men. These techniques are chosen because they counteract the usual emotional dysfunction of men and their tendency to do rather than to be. The quest for wholeness and liberation must include not only release from the prison of inherited gender stereotypes and self-expectations, but also an exploration of the human riches that lie buried deep inside men who have undertaken change.

Prayer

Several methods of centering prayer are known to the Christian spiritual tradition. Centering prayer is a structured way of being still in God's presence for an extended period of time. In centering prayer, the mind and body are both shut down as completely as possible and the soul is released to float in the presence of God, responding completely and spontaneously to God's enveloping love.

Centering prayer has three advantages for men in crisis. First, when done in the company of others, a sort of community is created of those who have shared being alone in God's presence. This type of intimate community is unknown to many men. Second, centering prayer does not depend on formulas, rules, or set patterns of words, beyond the possible use of The Jesus Prayer or a mantra in certain instances. Thus men are encouraged to turn loose of the security of "how it's always done" and to explore their own inner resources. Third, the incredible stillness of centering prayer balances the frenetic activity characterizing the lives of most men. A regular hour of total stillness and consuming love puts the stress and pressure that most men feel into a handleable perspective.

Centering prayer can be difficult and at times dangerous for the uninitiated, and so is usually taught by someone who is experienced in the regular personal use of centering prayer. The uninitiated man can find himself so deeply turned inward in the course of centering that he loses track of time and space or even the need to breathe. For this reason, centering prayer is practiced mostly in the company of others.

Guided Meditation

In addition to centering prayer, the classical techniques of guided meditation are of particular use in befriending men in crisis. Guided meditation is deceptive for men; it may look as if it is a form of doing, but it is actually a form of being. In the classical practice of guided meditation developed within the Benedictine tradition, a listener is asked to relax completely (in certain modern practice, relaxation is accompanied by massage). The listener then is taken verbally by the guide on an imaginary journey, perhaps through a tunnel into a castle where he wanders from room to room and describes his experience to the counseling guide as he goes. Finally, the guide leads the meditator into the presence of God or Christ, and asks the meditator to listen to what is being said to him. The meditator is then encouraged to remain in God's presence, to open up his feelings, and to let God's love wash over him. After resting there for a while, the meditator is brought slowly and carefully back to the present and then asked to reflect with the minister on his experience, including his feelings while in the presence of God.

Like centering prayer, guided meditation offers men in crisis an opportunity for liberation from the noise of patriarchy. First, it offers a time away from competition and one-upmanship, in a space where emotions are not so frightening and the pleasure of the task banishes momentary nervousness. Second, in doing a guided meditation, a man is called to trust his guide implicitly, for the meditator is placing himself in a highly vulnerable position. Third, most men committed to the Christian tradition feel comfortable in speaking of emotions in relation to God and Christ, even when they cannot speak of emotions in relation to other men. Guided meditation helps men find the seat of their feelings, to experience a variety of emotions normally repressed, and to practice the articulation of those emotions in relation to a socially acceptable subject. These experiences equip men better to express their emotions in other real-life settings.

Solidarity

Pastoral theologian Robert Katz outlines a method of empathy counseling
that bears many similarities to guided meditation, in that both techniques
involve the minister's readiness to enter deeply into the intimate spiritual
experiences of the meditator. Katz illustrates his point with this delightful
story, attributed to the eighteenth-century Hasidic master Rabbi Nachman
of Bratzlav:

> In a distant land, a prince lost his mind and imagined himself a rooster. He
> sought refuge under the table and lived there, naked, refusing to partake of the
> royal delicacies served in golden dishes — all he wanted and accepted was grain
> reserved for the roosters. The king was desperate. He sent for the best physi-
> cians, the most famous specialists: all admitted their incompetence. So did the
> magicians. And the monks, the ascetics, the miracle-makers, all their interven-
> tions proved fruitless. One day an unknown sage presented himself at court. "I
> think that I could heal the prince," he said shyly. "Will you allow me to try?"
> The king consented, and to the surprise of all present, the sage removed his
> clothes, and joining the prince under the table, began to crow like a rooster.
> Suspicious, the prince interrogated him: "Who are you and what are you doing
> here?" "And you," replied the sage, "who are you and what are you doing
> here?" "Can't you see? I am a rooster!" "Hmm," said the sage, "how very
> strange to meet you here!" "Why strange?" "You mean, you don't see? Really
> not? You don't see that I'm a rooster just like you?" The two men became
> friends and swore never to leave each other. And then the sage undertook to
> cure the prince by using himself as example. He started by putting on a shirt.
> The prince couldn't believe his eyes. "Are you crazy? Are you forgetting who
> you are? You really want to be a man?" "You know," said the sage in a gentle
> voice, "you mustn't ever believe that a rooster who dresses like a man ceases to
> be a rooster." The prince had to agree. The next day both dressed in a normal
> way. The sage sent for some dishes from the palace kitchen. "Wretch! What are
> you doing?" protested the prince, frightened in the extreme. "Are you going to
> eat like them now?" His friend allayed his fears: "Don't ever think that by eating
> like a man, at his table, a rooster ceases to be what he is; you mustn't ever be-
> lieve it is enough for a rooster to behave like a man to become human; you can
> do anything with man, in his world and even for him, and yet remain the
> rooster you are." And the prince was convinced; he resumed his life as a prince.
> (Katz 1985, 53–54)

The success of the sage's work with the young prince is premised upon the
sage's willingness to enter fully into the world in which the prince was living,
no matter how strange and uncomfortable it might have felt.

Community Building

A fourth form of spiritual direction available to men, and becoming rapidly
more popular in local parishes, is closed-boundary leaderless peer groups of
men who meet on a regular basis. This model is not to be confused with the
more traditional forms of activity that men have previously exercised, such as

men's prayer breakfasts. The style of these new groups allows men to meet with other men who are addressing a changing identity, having taken seriously women's demands for justice and equality, and to provide support and affirmation for each other in their struggle toward a new model of masculinity. The two most important operational principles of such groups is that they have closed boundaries (that is, they have exactly the same membership from week to week, rather than being open for drop-in visitors), and that they avoid the traditional patterns of male conversation, seeking instead to create a safe environment in which men may explore their deeper feelings with each other.

These groups began to catch on as much as ten years ago in churches abroad, but they have only recently begun to spring up in American congregations. Such groups assist ministers in two ways. First, they alleviate the minister of carrying an overpowering load, by creating a place to which ministers can refer men who wish to explore their own feelings and friendships with other men. Second, they create a place in which men can address together what frustrates them about the patriarchal character of the institutional church and thereby perhaps to secure their own position within the church, at least solidly on the peripheries, without the minister being put in the difficult position of defending the church to which he or she is committed. (Because information on these groups has been difficult to obtain, I have included some suggestions in my previous book, *New Adam: The Future of Male Spirituality*.)

LIBERATING MEN: A CHALLENGE

Men and women today are more and more aware of the importance of seeking healthier new ways of being. Not only do men need to be supported as they break the bonds of the powerful structures that unsettle and abuse them, but as well they need liberation from the crippling stereotypes of masculinity they have inherited. Images of the rugged pioneer, the burly woodsman, the Marlboro Man, the mentality of "one man against the odds," the disconnected and hedonistic Don Juan, all serve to alienate men from the care that can support them in their growth.

God loves us for who we are, not what we do. God loves people simply because they are human, created as a reflection of the divine image. God does not love them because of their résumés, their conquests, the connectedness of their femininity, or the ruggedness of their masculinity. For men to learn this will mean breaking the old shackles of gender-role definitions, and stilling many of the voices from their past that encouraged them to shut down their feelings, play tough, keep moving, push till it hurts.

Men need liberation from the expectations of who they are supposed to be and from the patriarchy that punishes them when they do not live up to the expectations. Within the institutional church, the need for men's liberation and a male liberation theology is not felt in the halls of power, nor will it be readily received there (unless to be readily co-opted there!), but it is the urgent need of the simple men in the community, the men who hurt alone and powerless, the disenfranchised men on the margins, and the men who have already turned their backs on the church as "simply one more instrument of alienation." In spite of women's sharp critique, many men are to be numbered among "the humble and meek," and it is to these men in crisis that the minister has much to offer.

The commission of the church has ever been to defend and renew the apostolic faith, but not to place it in a museum, or make it the darling of the conservative right, or use it as an escape from the painful realities of men's and women's daily living. The faith of the church is commanded to echo God's great cry to creation groaning: "See, the former things have come to pass, and new things I now declare; before they spring forth, I tell you of them" (Isa. 42:9); "See, I am making all things new" (Rev. 21:5). Christianity bears a long history of schism and heresy and yet the faith still nourishes millions of believing Christians throughout the world. The past can take care of itself; the power of The Tradition and the traditions is so great that they will continue to inform us, as long as the church takes seriously its ancient mission to study and teach. In the meantime, Scripture and the eyes of the faithful point ever to the future, in imitation of our God YHWH, whose name may be translated "I am in the process of becoming today what I will be for you tomorrow." The challenge to the creative minister today is to play out the exciting new possibilities of gender-specific caregiving.

BIBLIOGRAPHY

Adler, Alfred.
    1954   *Understanding Human Nature.* New York: Fawcett.
Agnon, Shemuel Yosef.
    1963   "The Kerchief." In *Great Jewish Short Stories*, ed. Saul Bellow, 142-54. New York: Dell.
Aristotle.
    1934   *The Nicomachean Ethics.* Trans. H. Rackham. London: William Heinemann Ltd. for the Loeb Classical Library.
Astrachan, Anthony.
    1986   *How Men Feel: Their Response to Women's Demands for Equality and Power.* Garden City, N.Y.: Doubleday.
Atwood, Margaret.
    1972   *Surfacing.* Don Mills, Ontario: PaperJacks.
Augsburger, David W.
    1986   *Pastoral Counseling across Cultures.* Philadelphia: Westminster.
Bly, Robert.
    1990   *Iron John: A Book about Men.* Reading, Mass.: Addison-Wesley.
Bograd, Michele.
    1990   "Women Treating Men." *Family Therapy Networker* (May-June):54-58.
Bowen, Murray.
    1990   *Family Therapy in Clinical Practice.* Northvale, N.J.: Jason Aronson.
Chodorow, Nancy.
    1978   *The Reproduction of Mothering.* Berkeley: University of California Press.
Clinebell, Charlotte.
    1976   *Counseling for Liberation.* Philadelphia: Fortress Press.
Culbertson, Philip.
    1992   *New Adam: The Future of Male Spirituality.* Minneapolis: Fortress Press.
    1993   "Men Dreaming of Men: Using Mitch Walker's 'Double Animus' in Pastoral Care." *Harvard Theological Review* 86, no. 2 (April): 219–32.
Culbertson, Philip, and Arthur Bradford Shippee.
    1990   *The Pastor: Readings from the Patristic Period.* Minneapolis: Fortress Press.
Doyle, James A.
    1989   *The Male Stress Syndrome.* 2d ed. Dubuque: William C. Brown.

Emerson, Gloria.
    1985   *Some American Men.* New York: Simon & Schuster.
Erkel, R. Todd.
    1990   "The Birth of a Movement." *Family Therapy Networker* (May-June):26-35.
Farrell, Warren.
    1986   *Why Men Are the Way They Are.* New York: McGraw-Hill.
    1991   "Men as Success Objects." *Utne Reader* (May-June):81-84.
Francke, Linda Bird.
    1983   "The Sons of Divorce." *New York Times Magazine* (May 22):40-41, 54-57.
Freire, Paulo.
    1970   *Pedagogy of the Oppressed.* Trans. Myra Bergman Ramis. New York: Herder and Herder.
Freud, Sigmund.
    1952   *On Dreams.* Trans. James Strachey. New York: W. W. Norton.
Friedman, Edwin.
    1985   *Generation to Generation: Family Process in Church and Synagogue.* New York: Guilford Press.
Gilligan, Carol.
    1982   *In a Different Voice: Psychological Theory and Women's Development.* Cambridge: Harvard University Press.
Gilmore, David.
    1990   *Manhood in the Making: Cultural Concepts of Masculinity.* New Haven: Yale University Press.
Griffiss, James.
    1985   *Anglican Theology and Pastoral Care.* Wilton: Morehouse-Barlow.
Healy, James.
    1992   "Man to Man: A Renewed Focus for Ministry." *Catholic World* (May-June):137-41.
Hopcke, Robert H.
    1990   *Men's Dreams, Men's Healing: A Psychotherapist Explores a New View of Masculinity through Jungian Dreamwork.* Boston and London: Shambhala.
    1991   *Jung, Jungians, and Homosexuality.* Boston and London: Shambhala.
Iglitzin, Lynne, and Ruth Ross, eds.
    1976   *Women in the World: A Comparative Study.* Santa Barbara, Calif.: ABC-CLIO.
Jacobs, John W.
    1982   "The Effect of Divorce on Fathers: An Overview of the Literature." *American Journal of Psychiatry* 139:1235-41.
Jung, Carl G.
    1973   *Memories, Dreams, Reflections.* Ed. Aniela Jaffe; trans. Richard and Clara Winston. Rev. ed. New York: Pantheon Books.
Junger, Sebastian.
    1992   "Hitting the Wall." *New York Times Magazine* (August 16):14.

Katz, Robert.
    1985   *Pastoral Care in the Jewish Tradition*. Philadelphia: Fortress.
Kimbrell, Andrew.
    1991   "A Time for Men to Pull Together." *Utne Reader* (May-June): 66-74.
Kübler-Ross, Elizabeth.
    1969   *On Death and Dying*. London: Tavistock.
Lawrence, D. H.
    1975   *Women in Love*. The Phoenix Edition. London: Heinemann.
Lederer, William, and Don Jackson.
    1968   *The Mirages of Marriage*. New York: W. W. Norton.
Letich, Larry.
    1991   "Do You Know Who Your Friends Are?" *Utne Reader* (May-June): 85-87.
Lewin, Tamar.
    1992   "Scary Monsters." *New York Times* (Oct):24, 26.
Miller, Jean Baker.
    1976   *Toward a New Psychology of Women*. Boston: Beacon Press.
Mitscherlich, Alexander.
    1969   *Society without the Father: A Contribution to Social Psychology*. New York: HarperCollins.
Myers, Michael.
    1989   *Men and Divorce*. New York: Guilford.
Noble, Lowell.
    1975   *Naked and Not Ashamed: An Anthropological, Biblical, and Psychological Study of Shame*. Jackson, Miss.: Jackson Printing.
Oates, Wayne E., and Charles E. Oates.
    1985   *People in Pain*. Philadelphia: Westminster.
O'Connor, Terrance.
    1990   "A Day for Men." *Family Therapy Networker* (May-June):36-39.
Patton, John.
    1985   *Is Human Forgiveness Possible?* Nashville: Abingdon.
Peter D. Hart Research Associates.
    1992   "Would You Give Up TV for a Millions Bucks?" *TV Guide* (October 10):10-17.
Pittman, Frank.
    1990   "The Masculine Mystique." *Family Therapy Networker* (May-June):40-52.
Pogrebin, Letty Cottin.
    1987   *Among Friends: Who We Like, Why We Like Them, and What We Do with Them*. New York: McGraw-Hill.
Radcliffe Richards, Janet.
    1980   *The Skeptical Feminist*. Boston: Routledge and Kegan Paul.
Rawlings, E., and D. K. Carter.
    1977   *Psychotherapy for Women*. Springfield, Ill.: Charles C. Thomas.

Rist, Darrell Yates.
  1992   "Born Gay?" *Nation* (October 19):424-29.
Rosenberg, Marshall B.
  1983   *A Model for Nonviolent Communication*. Philadelphia: New Society
          Publishers.
Sanders, Scott Russell.
  1991   "The Men We Carry in Our Minds . . . and How They Differ from
          the Real Lives of Most Men." *Utne Reader* (May-June):76-78.
Scarf, Maggie.
  1987   *Intimate Partners: Patterns in Love and Marriage*. New York:
          Random House.
Tannen, Deborah.
  1990   *You Just Don't Understand: Women and Men in Conversation*. New
          York: Ballentine.
Tavris, Carol.
  1992   *The Mismeasure of Woman: Why Women Are Not the Better Sex, the
          Inferior Sex, or the Opposite Sex*. New York: Simon & Schuster.
Thistlethwaite, Susan Brooks.
  1992   "Great White Fathers." *Christianity and Crisis* (January 13):416-18.
Thurston, Bonnie Bowman.
  1989   *The Widows: A Women's Ministry in the Early Church*. Minneapolis:
          Fortress.
Tiger, Lionel.
  1969   *Men in Groups*. New York: Random House.
Updike, John.
  1968   *Couples*. Middlesex: Penguin Books.
Viorst, Judith.
  1986   *Necessary Losses: The Loves, Illusions, Dependencies and Impossible Ex-
          pectations that All of Us Have to Give Up in Order to Grow*. New York:
          Simon & Schuster.
Wakefield, Dan.
  1988   "Common Men at Prayer," *New York Times Magazine* (April 3):
          14, 16.
Witkin-Lanoil, Georgia.
  1986   *The Male Stress Syndrome*. New York: Newmarket Press.